Douglas DC-9

ARTHUR PEARCY

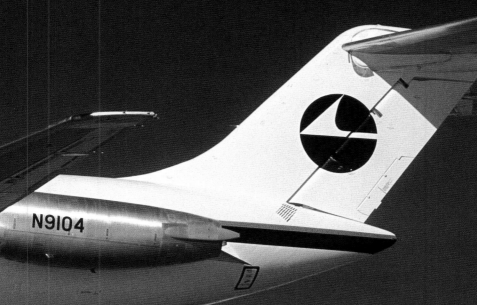

N9I04

Acknowledgements

The Author wishes to thank the many airlines which supplied photographs, and special thanks to Harry Gann, Manager, Aircraft Information with the Douglas Aircraft Company at Long Beach, California who devoted many hours sorting out many of the transparencies used in this book.

Copyright © 1993 by Arthur Pearcy

First published in the UK in 1994 by
Airlife Publishing Ltd

British Library Cataloguing in Publication Data
A catalogue record for this book
is available from the British Library

ISBN 1 85310 359 4

Printed and bound in Hong Kong by World Print Ltd.

Airlife Publishing Ltd

101 Longden Road, Shrewsbury SY3 9EB

Introduction

The Douglas DC-9, designed and manufactured by the Douglas Aircraft Company located at Long Beach, California, is still today one of the world's most popular twin-jet airliners with 976 delivered by October 1982, when the last aircraft was completed for the US Navy. Making its maiden flight on 25 February 1965, it was the last civil airliner to be designed exclusively by the Douglas company before it became part of the huge McDonnell Douglas Corporation in 1967. Today over 900 DC-9s are still in service including some of the first production models.

In the early 1960s Delta Air Lines became increasingly interested in helping to develop a small jetliner that would replace the Convair Cv-440 on shorter segments and also enable the company to move towards an all-jet fleet. During 1960/61 a series of discussions were conducted with Ed Burton, Vice-President of engineering at Douglas, leading ultimately to the creation of the DC-9. Delta proved that traffic levels in small cities were already outgrowing the capacities of their current twin-engined airliners. Delta persuaded Donald W Douglas Snr to visit their founder, Collett Everman Woolman at Atlanta; this resulting in a preliminary letter of intent, signed by Woolman on 13 March 1963, to purchase fifteen DC-9s at a unit price slightly in excess of $3 million, Douglas subsequently failed an attempt to secure an order from American Airlines, but decided to go into production. The Delta offer was accepted on 16 April 1963.

On 12 January 1965, the first aircraft was rolled out at Long Beach, and on 25 February, a month ahead of schedule, the DC-9 c/n 45696 f/n 1 N9DC took-off on its initial test flight. Five aircraft were used in an extensive test programme conducted by twelve pilots, and by 8 September, three months ahead of estimation, the first DC-9 was ready to be accepted by Delta. On 7 October christened *Delta Prince* with a bottle of water from the twenty cities that it would serve, DC-9-14 c/n 45699 f/n 8 flew to Atlanta on delivery to Delta. Official FAA certification followed on 23 November, again ahead of schedule, and on 3 December Delta introduced the DC-9 into commercial service. By 1970 the airline possessed seventy-five DC-9s consisting of seventeen Series 14 and fifty-eight Series 32.

Five major versions of the trim, high T-tail DC-9 twin-jet were developed with the Series 10 being the first model of this versatile, short to medium range transport to enter airline service. Sound, basic transportation designed traditionally has a way of growing as was the case with the DC-9. The Series 30, the most popular version, was built with a longer fuselage and a high-lift wing system of leading-edge slats for excellent short-field performance. The Series 30 was followed by the still larger Series 40, having the wings of the Series 30 and higher thrust engines. The Series 20, the fourth in the family, combined the short fuselage of the Series 10 with the high-lift wing developed for the Series 30 and the higher power-producing fan jet engines of the Series 40 for operation from shorter runways.

The Series 50, with an additionally long fuselage stretch over the Series 40, had wings similar to the Series 30, and still more powerful engines, being designed to meet growing demands on shorter range routes and to continue the reliable performance of previous versions. It offered extra capacity and lower break-even costs, particularly over high density routes, and had a high degree of commonality with the systems and components of earlier DC-9s.

The Series 30 met with considerable success, accounting in its civil and military guise for two out of every three DC-9s built. With operating costs only marginally higher than those of the Series 10, but carrying up to twenty-five more passengers, the Series 30 achieved remarkably low seat-mile costs, especially over short sectors. The Series 20 and 40 were developed to meet specific requirements for SAS for its intra-Scandinavian network. The Series 20 was intended to operate in and out of smaller airfields with relatively short runways, whilst the Series 40 was a short-range, high-capacity transport. The Series 20 combined the fuselage and capacity of the Series 10 with the long-span wing of the Series 30, complete with leading-edge slats and double slotted flaps. It was acquired only by SAS which accepted them between December 1968 and May 1969. The Series 40 traded range and airfield length requirements for higher seating capacity and payload. The fuselage was stretched by 6 ft 2 in over the Series 30 to 125 ft and it seated up to 125 passengers in a high-density configuration. SAS initially ordered ten DC-9-41s later increased to cover a total of forty-nine airliners. Japan Air System, ex-Toa Domestic Airlines, became the second and only other customer for this version when it ordered fourteen DC-9-41s, later increased to twenty-two for its dense, high-frequency, inter-island services.

The DC-9 is forecast to remain in service, alongside the equally successful MD-80 Series until the turn of the century and after.

DOUGLAS DC-9 SPECIFICATIONS					
	Series 10	Series 20	Series 30	Series 40	Series 50
First flight	25 Feb 1965	18 Sep 1968	1 Aug 1966	28 Nov 1967	17 Dec 1974
Wing span ft/in metres	89 4 27.25	93 5 28.47	93 4 28.47	93 4 28.47	93 4 28.47
Length ft/in metres	104 4 31.82	104 4 31.82	119 3 36.39	125 6 38.28	133 6 40.72
Height ft/in metres	27 5 8.38	27 5 8.38	27 5 8.38	28 0 8.53	28 0 8.53
Wing area sq/ft sq/metres	934.3 86.8	1000.7 92.97	1000.7 92.97	1000.7 92.97	1000.7 92.97
Max t/o weight lbs/ k/g	90,700 41,141	100,000 45,359	110,000 49,885	114,000 51,709	121,000 54,884
Max cruise speed mph km/hr	561 903	570 917	570 917	558 898	558 898
Max range miles km	2,000 3,219	1,910 3,073	1,635 2,631	1,750 2,816	1,635 2,631
Engines (two) Pratt & Whitney Thrust lbs.	JT8D-7 14,000	JT8D-11 15,000	JT8D-15 15,500	JT8D-11/ 15/17 15,000/15,500/ 16,000	JT8D-17 16,000
First delivery customer/date	Delta 4 Dec 1965	SAS 11 Dec 1968	Eastern 22 Feb 1967	SAS 29 Feb 1968	Swissair 14 Aug 1975
Number built	137	10	662	71	96

ABX AIR INC (GB/ABX)   United States of America

Airborne Express is the operating name of ABX Air, a leading US small-package express and freight forwarding company formed on 17 April 1980. Operations commenced later in that year. It is a subsidiary of the Seattle-based Airborne Freight, this resulting from the merger of Midwest Charter Express into Airborne Express, adopting the latter name. The current title was adopted so as to avoid confusion between the airline name and the names of the parent company and its trade name.

The company provides an extensive network of overnight express small-package services from its hub located at the Air Park, Wilmington, Ohio, throughout the United States, and to no less than 183 countries worldwide. Every night of the week, the Airborne Express fleet of all-cargo Douglas DC-9 aircraft converge on the operator's Wilmington, Ohio, hub, where packages are sorted and transferred to flights bound for some ninety destinations spread across the USA. Expansion north into Canada and south to Mexico are currently being planned, whilst apparently plans are in hand to 'hush-kit' the Douglas DC-9s. The company employs 3,500 personnel, and more of the versatile and useful work-horse, the DC-9, are being sought from a second-hand market which has waiting list for the type.

The Airborne Express fleet is largely composed of Douglas twin-jet aircraft; the McDonnell Douglas aircraft listing for 31 March 1992, listed forty-six DC-9s and twenty-three DC-8s on inventory. The fleet consists of a rare assortment of quite rare DC-9 aircraft these including the Series -11, -15, -31, -32, -32CF, -33F, -33RC, -33CF and -41, the latter including two acquired from Japan Air System and are N951AX c/n 47616 f/n 759 ex-JA8433: N952AX c/n 47615 f/n 751 ex-JA8432 whilst during March 1992 N967AX c/n 47509 f/n 643 ex-SE-DAO came from Sweden. At least eight DC-9-31s came from Australia, one -33F came from Switzerland, one -33RC from Jugoslavia, one -32 from Spain, whilst others came from United States operators. The early -11 and -14 aircraft came from Italy.

The livery adopted by Airborne Express for its DC-9 fleet includes a very pale blue/grey aircraft for the top and sides, with a pale grey lower surface. The tail unit has an attractive red panel with blue pinstripes above and below, this being at an angle. The 'AIRBORNE EXPRESS' title on the fuselage top has the first two letters of each word in red, the rest being dark blue or black. The aircraft registration is on the rear of the fuselage near the tail unit and is black.

Depicted is DC-9-32 N908AX c/n 47008 f/n 98 ex-VH-TJK and is one of a number of Australian DC-9s used by the company, a further two being DC-9-31s and identified as N906AX c/n 47072 f/n 270 ex-VH-TJM and N907AX c/n 47203 f/n 401 ex-VH-TJN. *(ECMS)*

ADRIA AIRWAYS (JP/ADR)   Jugoslavia

Adria Airways was formed in 1961 with that title, but was re-organised during 1968 as part of the Interexport group, when the name was changed to Inex Adria Airways. In May 1968, the title was changed back to Adria Airways when the airline became independent. With international recognition of its new Slovenian state, Adria has resumed some of its former operations after reviewing the situation plus its airline fleet structure. The carrier successfully operated charter and scheduled services between Jugoslavia, Europe, the Middle East and North Africa. Scheduled domestic services were also operated between major cities in Jugoslavia and the Adriatic coast resorts. International scheduled services were operated to Larnaca, Athens, Bari, Munich, London (Gatwick), Paris, Tel Aviv, Vienna, Frankfurt and Moscow.

As of March 1992 the Adria fleet consisted of three Airbus 320s, two Douglas DC-9-32s, one DC-9-33, one MD-81, four MD-82s, and two de Havilland Dash 7 aircraft. The airline accepted the first of two DC-9-32s YU-AHJ c/n 47239 f/n 466 on 25 April 1969, this being destined for delivery to Alitalia as I-DIZE but was cancelled.

European operations out of Ljubljana were commenced with the 110-passenger twin-jets to Belgrade, initially in 1970. Since then, Adria has operated a total of twelve different DC-9-32/33CFs and two DC-9-51s, the latter being 115-seat aircraft. Services with the airline link Ljubljana, Belgrade, Sarajevo, Skopje, Maribor and Zagreb. Package tour flights are successful whilst contract charters carry migrant workers between Jugoslavia and Germany.

A new livery now adorns the Adria fleet which consists of the title "ADRIA" styled in black across the aircraft in large letters. The aircraft is white overall and the tail unit has a heart design in black, this being on its side with two black bars across. The Jugoslav national flag is painted on the base of the fin, and the aircraft registration is black on the rear fuselage top. The engine nacelles are white with 'DC-9' inscribed. Depicted is DC-9-32 YU-AJF c/n 47570 f/n 684 delivered to Adria on 16 May 1973, and is today still in service. *(MAP)*

AERO CALIFORNIA (JR/ACL/ZCA)   Mexico

Aero California is a Mexican regional carrier, operating scheduled passenger services linking Mexico City, Colima, Culiacan, Guadalajora, Las Mochis, Tijuana, La Paz, Ciudad Obregon and Hermosillo. Operations commenced in 1960 from its headquarters located at Baja California Sur, Mexico, near the border with the United States. It currently has a varied fleet consisting of a single Cessna 402C, one Beech C-45H, one Douglas DC-3, and nine Douglas DC-9-14/15 twin-jet airliners.

The airline operates scheduled flights in western Mexico serving primarily the popular commercial and tourist centres located in the beautiful Baja California and Gulf of California resort areas. The DC-9-10 was first introduced on its routes during June 1982, and it later leased four DC-9-14/15s from Guinness Peat Aviation and one DC-9-15MC which had previously been operated by Texas International.

Other destinations served by Aero California include Muleje, Loreto, Guaymas and Cabo San Lucas. Of its current fleet of Douglas DC-9s eight are leased from Guinness Peat, one from

Intercredit and one from Polaris. Plans are said to be in hand to lease further DC-9-15s for an expanded network. Employees currently number 300. A veteran in the fleet is DC-9-14 XA — RXG c/n 45714 f/n 7 previously registered N651TX.

The Aero California DC-9 livery is bright and styled on a four-colour band which is wrapped around the centre of the fuselage and diagonally across the tail unit. The colours range from a pale yellow to deep red and colours from this band form a pin-stripe line down the lower fuselage and vertically up the tail unit. An all-white fuselage carries the title 'AERO CALIFORNIA' in black on the top aft of the cockpit, and the aircraft registration is carried on the rear fuselage forward of the tail unit. The engine nacelles are white but include the bright colours used on the fuselage and tail. Depicted is DC-9-15 XA-RKT c/n 47122 f/n 224 ex-EI-BZZ and on lease from Guinness Peat Aviation. This airliner was initially delivered on 20 December 1967, to Aeronaves de Mexico and registered XA-SOD and named *Tamaulipas*. In February 1972 the title of the airline was changed to Aeromexico. *(MAP)*

AERO LLOYD (LL/AEF/XLL)   Germany

Aero Lloyd (Flugreisen Luftverkens KG) was founded on 5 December 1980, and commenced flying operations in March 1981, initially with a small fleet of three French Se.210 Cravelle airliners. In May 1982, the first Douglas DC-9-32 was acquired by this Frankfurt-based airline and since then the fleet has been considerably increased and today it has an all McDonnell Douglas fleet. Scheduled services were introduced on 31 October 1988.

This German carrier operates passenger charter flights from Berlin, Bremen, Düsseldorf, Frankfurt, Hamburg, Hannover, Koln (Cologne), Munich, Münster, Nurnberg, Saarbrucken and Stuttgart to the popular holiday resorts on the Mediterranean and Canary Islands, and to the Middle East. The company operates scheduled domestic services from Frankfurt to Berlin/Tegel. The major shareholders are Air Charter Market, Dipl Kfm Reinhold Braumer and Jan Klimitz.

The airline has aimed, with some success, to undercut the air fares charged by Lufthansa. On 1 December 1989, a Munich to London (Gatwick) service was inaugurated. The McDonnell Douglas aircraft inventory dated 31 December 1991, lists three MDC DC-8-63s, three DC-9-32s, twelve MD-83s and four MD-87 airliners. The three DC-9-32 twin-jet airliners came from Garuda in Indonesia and are D-ALLA c/n 47673 f/n 779 ex-PK-GNK: D-ALLB c/n 47680 f/n 781 ex-PK-GNL 'and D-ALLC c/n 47672 f/n 778 ex-PK-GNJ. Th first DC-9-32 flew with the Frankfurt-based airline in May 1982, and the Long Beach records reveal that D-ALLA had flown 16,166 hours and completed 11,251 landings up to delivery to Aero Lloyd on 9 March 1982. D-ALLB had similarly flown 15,533 hours and completed 10,701 landings and D-ALLC 16,073 hours and 11,192 landings, the latter being delivered to Aero Lloyd from Garuda on 15 March 1982.

The livery of Aero Lloyd consists of a three-colour — gold/orange/red — fuselage band positioned below the windowline, extending from nose to tail. This is broken by the title 'AERO LLOYD' in black on the forward fuselage, a fuselage which is white to wing level than natural metal below. The white tail unit is decorated with the three fuselage colours of gold/orange/red, angled at forty-five degrees with the airline title 'AERO LLOYD' in black. A small German national flag appears near the top of the tail unit. The engine nacelles are white decorated by the gold/orange/red cheatline, while the aircraft registration is positioned over the rear windows on the fuselage. Depicted is Douglas DC-9-32 D-ALLA c/n 47673 f/n 779 delivered to Aero Lloyd on 9 March 1982 and today is still in service. (MDC)

AEROMEXICO (AM/AMX)   Mexico

Aerovias de Mexico SA is today one of the two national airlines operating in the second most populous country in Latin America. It was established as early as 1934 as Aeronaves de Mexico, and commenced operating between Mexico City and Acapulco in September 1934. Since 1952, several smaller Mexican airlines have been taken over including Lineas Aereas Mineras (LAMSA), Aerovias Reforma, Aerolineas Mexicanas and Guest Aerovias. In 1959, the airline was nationalised and the Pan American holding passed to the Mexican government. During 1970, under a Mexican government plan, the domestic airlines in Mexico were rationalised into an integrated air transport system under the control of Aeronaves de Mexico and organised into eight smaller carriers. In February 1972 the current Aeromexico title was adopted, and in April 1988 the airline was declared bankrupt by the Mexican government, the owner. After a six-month recovery programme, services were re-introduced to thirty domestic destinations and five cities in the United States. In November 1988, a 65 per cent controlling stake in the airline was acquired by Groupo Dictum, a consortium of Mexican business interests. The Mexican pilots' union, ASPA, purchased the remaining shares. After just one year of private operation, the airline became profitable.

For many years Aeromexico has operated products built by the Douglas Aircraft Company located at Long Beach. These included the DC-8 now withdrawn from service, whilst currently the Douglas DC-9, DC-10 and MD-80 airliners are on the inventory, although orders for the Boeing 757 and 767 are pending. In December 1989, the airline accepted the first of ten MD-88 twin-jet airliners which are supported by fifteen DC-9-32s plus ten MD-82s. Most of the Douglas fleet are leased from the Guinness Peat Aviation organisation.

The latest Aeromexico livery, introduced in the early 1980s is bright and attractive consisting of a highly-polished natural metal fuselage and wings, this forming a backdrop for the broad very bright orange cheatline. This also saves a considerable amount of weight, and subsequently saves fuel. The famous Mexican bird-man motif appears in white on the all-orange tail unit, with the aircraft registration in white on the fuselage at the base of the tail. The 'aeromexico' title is in white and appears on the broad fuselage cheatline below the windowline. A small Mexican national flag appears on the forward fuselage above the cheatline. The engine nacelles are in orange.

Depicted is DC-9-15 XA-SOA c/n 47059 f/n 125 seen at Mexico City in the new Aeromexico livery with a Douglas DC-10 in the background. The airliner was delivered on 29 May 1967, as XA-PIK when the company was titled Aeronaves de Mexico. (MAP)

AIR CANADA (AC/ACA)

Canada

Air Canada is the Canadian international air carrier providing scheduled services plus charter passenger and cargo flights. This, the largest Canadian airline was founded on 10 April 1937, as Trans-Canada Airlines by the Canadian government with the stock vested in Canadian National Railways. On 7 July the first survey flight was made from Vancouver to Seattle whilst Trans-Canada express cargo flights started on 17 October 1938, air mail on the first day of December and passenger services on 1 April 1939.

The early TCA fleet consisted of Lockheed Electras, while Lockheed 14s were added in 1940. Extensions to the network quickly took place operating to Moncton, New Brunswick on 15 February 1940, to Halifax, Nova Scotia on 1 April 1941, and most important of all to New York on 10 May 1941. By the time the airline commenced the trans-Atlantic services on 1 May 1947, TCA had a comprehensive network of routes throughout Canada, All overseas routes were operated by the Rolls-Royce-engined Canadair DC-4M 'North Star' manufactured in Canada, but they proved to be uncompetitive and Lockheed Super Constellations were introduced on the trans-Atlantic route by 14 May 1954. The airline became the first operator of the turboprop aircraft in the American continent when the Vickers Viscount was introduced on 1 April 1955.

In 1965 the name of the airline was changed by Act of Parliament from TCA to Air Canada, and it became one of the first Douglas DC-9 operators when it took delivery of a DC-9-14 CF-TLB c/n 45711 f/n 4 on 12 April 1966. A total of six -14 series were purchased new from Long Beach, joined later by nine ex-Continental DC-9-15RC aircraft plus forty-five of the larger DC-9-32, for use on its domestic trunk and regional routes to the United States and the Caribbean. Today a fleet of thirty-five DC-9-32s configured to carry 100 passengers remain in service, being used within Canada on routes serving Calgary, Charlottetown, Edmonton, Fredericton, Halifax, Moncton, Montreal, Quebec, Regina and St. John, as well as to points over the border to the United States. As of 1991 the Air Canada Douglas DC-9 fleet had recorded in excess of two million landings.

The Air Canada livery has been in use since 1977 and features a bright red or crimson cheatline covering the windowline with a similar bright coloured tail unit. The national maple leaf flag of Canada appears in white in a white circle on the tail. 'AIR CANADA' titles are carried on the forward upper fuselage in red, along with a small maple leaf replica. The upper surface of the aircraft is white from wing level, the lower and underneath being natural metal, as are the engine nacelles. The registration is in black on the red cheatline forward of the engines, and the Air Canada fleet number is carried at the top of the fin in white. Depicted is DC-9-32 C-FLTJ c/n 47019 f/n 113 Fleet No. 709. *(Chris Doggett)*.

The airline was one of the very first DC-9 operators and took delivery of its second DC-9-14 CF-TLB c/n 45711 f/n 4 on 12 April 1966. The DC-9 CF-TLC had also been registered N1792U and later became OH-LYB.

AIR FLORIDA

United States of America

Air Florida, a wholly-owned subsidary of Air Florida System, commenced operations on 29 September 1972, as a carrier based in Miami. Following deregulations in 1978, the airline operated scheduled passenger and cargo services to more than fifty destinations in Florida, the north eastern and south eastern United States, the Caribbean, central America and Europe. The airline became affiliated with feeder services within Florida and to points in the Bahamas under the title Air Florida Commutor introduced in 1981.

A very colourful airline, Air Florida had on its inventory in March 1984, one Douglas DC-10-30, fourteen Boeing 737-200, two 737-100 and had three new 757-200 on order with Boeing. The six DC-9-15F/RC aircraft which were put into service on 10 June 1977, replaced earlier Lockheed Electra turboprop airliners. It employed nearly 2,000 personnel. Other DC-9 twin-jet airliners were leased from time to time and the type remained in service until 1981/82.

However, the airline's history was plagued by financial difficulties, which finally forced the company to file for protection under Chapter 11 of the US Federal bankruptcy code on 3 July 1984. Part of the Air Florida fleet and route network were subsequently acquired by Midway Airlines, whilst three DC-9s went to Ross Aviation.

The Air Florida livery was bright with a sunshine-orange fuselage top; this orange also including all but the trailing edge of the tail unit which was sky blue. A styled 'af' in white appeared on the tail and 'air florida' in white on the fuselage top. A blue cheatline covered the windowline being broader on the nose section, and the engine nacelles were also in blue carrying the aircraft registration in white. By the cockpit a red design included a bird in flight in white. The underside of the aircraft was light grey.

It is coincidental that most of the Air Florida DC-9-15RC aircraft were originally delivered to Continental, then sold to Air Canada prior to sale or lease to Air Florida. These included N50AF c/n 47010 f/n 97: N60AF c/n 47011 f/n 102: N73AF c/n 47152 f/n 170: N29AF c/n 45826 f/n 79. Today the three used by Ross Aviation are used on US Government contracts working primarily for the Energy Research & Development Administration (ERDA).

Depicted in landing sequence is DC-9-15RC N70AF of Air Florida c/n 47014 f/n 141 initially delivered to Continental as N8906 on 23 July 1967. Today it is still in service, as N561PC with Emery Worldwide. *(MAP)*

AIR JAMAICA (JM/AJM)

Jamaica

Air Jamaica was formed in October 1968, by the Government of Jamaica and Air Canada with operations commencing on 1 April 1969. During 1980 the airline became fully state-owned with the Jamaican Government remaining as the one hundred per cent shareholder. The airline offers a scheduled passenger and cargo service linking Kingston and Montego Bay with such points as Curacao, Grand Cayman, Nassau, plus points in the United States including Atlanta, Baltimore, Los Angeles, Miami, New York and Philadelphia. Direct services to London (Heathrow) are operated jointly with British Airways, whilst a service to Toronto is likewise operated jointly with Air Canada.

Prior to commencing operations, Air Jamaica purchased two DC-9-32s from Douglas at Long Beach, these being 6Y-JGA c/n 47351 f/n 442 initially delivered to Air Canada as CF-TMM on 23 January 1969, going to Air Jamaica on 7 March. Likewise 6Y-JGB c/n 47352 f/n 453 went initially to Air Canada as CF-TMN on 18 February 1969, and to Air Jamaica on 27 March. A third DC-9-32 6Y-JIJ c/n 47639 f/n 735 joined the fleet on 28 June 1974, direct from the factory. The Douglas twin-jet airliners flew schedules on the airline's important US routes serving Miami and New York from both Kingston and Montego Bay, and to various points in the Caribbean.

The first two DC-9s were eventually sold to US Air on 19 November 1980, whilst 6Y-JIJ continued in service until November 1982. This aircraft was leased to ALM Antillean Airlines as PJ-SND in June 1977 and April 1980. The bright livery adopted by Air Jamaica typifies the warmth of the Caribbean with the DC-9s having a tri-colour finish of yellow, orange and white. The orange covered the windowline. The lower portion of the aircraft was grey. The yellow and orange swept up to the tail unit broadening with an airline logo in an orange disc appearing on the tail. The title 'air jamaica' was placed on the white of the tri-colour cheatline on the forward lower fuselage, and the Jamaican national flag appeared on the white engine nacelles. The aircraft registration in black appeared on the white cheatline. Depicted is the third Air Jamaica DC-9-32 6Y-JIJ. *(MAP)*

AIR WEST

United States of America

Air West was formed by the merger of Pacific Airlines, Bonanza Airlines and West Coast Airlines on 9 April 1968. In 1966 statistics revealed that some of the thirteen Local Service Airlines in the USA were lagging behind the industry leaders by quite a large margin, both in traffic and financially. There were many mergers and in June 1967 Pacific Airlines discussed the merger subject with West Coast. However in August 1967 an enlarged merger proposal involved Pacific, West Coast and Bonanza and on 9 April 1968, a new airline, Air West, received approval from President Lyndon B. Johnson, this being necessary because of foreign routes involved.

The US airline fleet listing for 31 December 1969, reveals that the Air West inventory consisted of four Douglas DC-9-10, fifteen DC-9-30 and thirty-three Fairchild-Hiller FH-227 airliners. The McDonnell Douglas archives reveal that the first Air West DC-9, a Series 31 N9330 c/n 47138 f/n 318 was delivered to the new airline at its San Francisco headquarters on 27 May 1968. From Bonanza and West Coast the new airline inherited a fleet of DC-9s which comprised eight DC-9-11/14s and one single DC-9-31. The

remnant from a Bonanza order for the larger Douglas twin-jet airliners was delivered from Long Beach in Air West livery resulting in the DC-9-31 fleet being built up to sixteen aircraft within a very short period of time.

Unfortunately Air West existed for only three years, being purchased by the huge Hughes Air Corporation on 3 April 1970, and renamed Hughes Air West. As Air West the airline had incurred heavy losses, due largely to operating expensive jet airliners on routes which were far too short to be economic. One such route was of only eleven miles or eighteen kilometres.

The livery of Air West was simple and carried on an all-white fuselage, the tail unit being equally divided with red lower, and the top-half mustard. The title 'AIR WEST' appeared stepped on the border of the tail colours. AIR WEST in mustard and red alternatively was carried on the forward fuselage below the windowline. The registration was in red on the all-white engine nacelles. Depicted is a trio of DC-9-3s including N9335 c/n 47337 f/n 415 delivered to Air West on 27 November 1968, and seen on a pre-delivery test flight from the Long Beach factory. (MDC)

ALITALIA (AZ/AZA)

Italy

Linee Aeree Italiane (Alitalia) was formed on 16 September 1946. Of the two defeated Axis powers, Italy finished World War 2 as a non-belligerent and as a result was able to re-establish its civil air transport industry more quickly than Germany. The two largest companies to be formed in Italy were Aerolinee Italiane Internazionali (Alitalia) associated with British European Airways which held thirty per cent of the shares, and Linee Aeree Italiane (LAI) associated with TWA in the United States, which held a forty per cent interest. The two airlines merged on 1 September 1957. The initial Alitalia fleet consisted of Fiat G.12s, Sovia Marchetti SM.95s and Avro Lancastrians which were replaced the following year by Douglas DC-4 Skymasters on the main routes. Both airlines had had a long history of operating both Douglas and McDonnell Douglas transport aircraft, and over the years Alitalia has operated the Douglas DC-3, DC-4, DC-6, DC-7, DC-8, DC-9, DC-10 and more recently the MD-82 and the new MD-11 airliner.

Today Alitalia and its subsidiary Aero Transporti Italiani (ATI), operate the largest fleet of Long Beach-built twin-jet airliners of any operator outside the United States. It has been a prolific Douglas DC-9 operator since it acquired the first of its DC-9-32s on 8 August 1967, this being I-DIKA c/n 47038 f/n 136. Three all-

cargo DC-9-32F aircraft were first introduced in May 1968, two of these being I-DIKF c/n 47220 f/n 296 and I-DIKG c/n 47221 f/n 305 the latter being sold to the US Navy on 1 August 1984, becoming BuNo.163037 with 29,087 hours and 28,067 landings.

The Alitalia fleet of twin-jet airliners operates an extensive European and domestic network taking in thirteen cities in Italy and thirty-two in Europe. Manchester is just one of the airports in the United Kingdom on the regular schedule of Alitalia DC-9 airliners. The Italian national airline today operates a worldwide network of scheduled passenger and cargo flights from Milan and Rome serving Europe, North and South America, the Middle and Far East, north-east and South Africa and Australia. These are in addition to the extensive network of domestic services already mentioned.

Livery of Alitalia consists of an overall white airliner, with a large styled 'A' with red insert on the tail unit, this being very dark green like the title 'Alitalia' on the top of the fuselage, the 'A' having also a red insert. A broad dark green cheatline covers the windowline extending from nose to tail and joining the large 'A' on the tail. The last two letters of the registration are carried on the top of the fin. Depicted is DC-9-32 I-DIKS c/n 47229 f/n 356 delivered to Alitalia on 8 August 1968. *(MAP)*

ALLEGHENY AIRLINES   United States of America

Allegheny Airlines was founded during 1937 as All-American Airlines, and began an experimental mail pick-up service on 13 September 1938, over a network of routes radiating from Pittsburgh, Pennsylvania. During 1951 the name was changed to Allegheny Airlines, and by this time the airline had become a normal certificated local carrier. In October 1959 the airline introduced the popular Convair Cv.340 airliner on a new and unique kind of service which considerably increased load factors. The customer bought a ticket at the airport, wrote his/her name on it and had it date and time stamped. The passengers were allowed on the aircraft in order of the time stamp, and only about five per cent of the passengers were refused a seat, and the successful ones received a thirty-six per cent discount below the normal fare. In February 1960 Allegheny ordered five Convair Cv.540s powered by British-built Napier Eland propeller turbine engines.

On 14 March 1968, Lake Central Airlines merged with Allehgeny after approval from the shareholders and the Civil Aeronautics Board (CAB). The US airline fleet listing for 31 December 1969, revealed that the Allegheny fleet consisted of forty-two Convair Cv.580/660 aircraft and twenty-four Douglas DC-9-30 twin-jet airliners. The airline had placed the DC-9 in service on 1 September 1966, testing the market with a single DC-9-14 N6140A c/n 47049 f/n 42 delivered to Allegheny on 29 July. This was supplemented the following year with the first of a fleet of Douglas DC-9-31/32 airliners fitted out to carry 110 passengers. The first DC-9-31 was N970VJ c/n 47050 f/n 118 delivered on 2 June 1967, and this aircraft is still in service today with US Air. Deliveries of the Long Beach product extended well into 1979 and included a number DC-9-51s. An order for eight new DC-9-51s was placed with Douglas in June 1974. On 28 October 1979, Allegheny became US Air which today and several acquisitions later is one of the world's largest airlines.

The Allegheny livery consisted of an overall white fuselage upper surface, with a windowline dark blue band which broadened as it reached the rear of the DC-9. The all-white tail unit carried the airline's arrow symbol in red and dark blue, this being repeated on the forward top fuselage followed by the 'ALLEGHENY' title in red. The registration in white was carried on the dark blue engine nacelles. A white pinstripe was painted below the dark blue fuselage line, the lower fuselage remaining natural metal. The name 'Vistajet' was inscribed in red below the cockpit.

Depicted is DC-9-31 N972VJ c/n 47052 f/n 142 delivered to the airline on 28 July 1967, which today is still operating with the huge US Air fleet. At some period it carried the registration N6143A. The DC-9 is seen during a pre-delivery test flight over the Long Beach port facility adjacent to the Douglas factory. (MDC)

ALL STAR AIRLINES

United States of America

All Star received its operating certificate on 1 April 1983, and commenced charter services with two Douglas DC-9-10 twin-jet airliners. It was based at Woburn, Massachusetts, and by March 1985, had increased its fleet to three DC-9-10s and had ninety-five employees. Unfortunately the airline only lasted for just over two years, ceasing all flight operations on 29 October 1985. In that time it had provided inclusive tour (IT) flights to gambling resorts located in Atlantic City, Reno and others located in Florida and the Caribbean.

The fleet of three DC-9-14/15F airliners were leased to All Star and the airline livery was quite unusual and very colourful. The top of the fuselage was light blue forward, this being inter-changed by a white portion which broadened to the tail. The tail unit was divided equally horizontally into a blue and red portion.

The latter red colour was a continuation of the fuselage cheatline which followed the windowline. On this cheatline was the aircraft registration in white forward of the engine nacelles which were natural metal but carried a blue and red stripe surround divided by a white pinstripe. A styled airline title 'All star' appeared red on the blue fuselage top with a white star dividing the two words.

Depicted is DC-9-15RC N73AF c/n 47152 f/n 170 which had a very chequered career before being initially delivered to Continental Air Lines on 22 September 1967, as N8908. On 1 May 1973, it was sold to Air Canada becoming CF-TOU and then followed a series of leases to Air Florida and returns to Air Canada. It was N65AF with Air Florida with the exchanges lasting until at least March 1980. *(MAP)*

ALM —
ANTILLEAN AIRLINES (LM/ALM)

Netherlands Antilles

ALM Antillean Airlines (Antilliaanse Luchtvaart Maatschappij) was formed in 1964 to take over the services of the Caribbean division of KLM Royal Dutch Airlines. Operations commenced during August 1964. On 1 January 1969, ALM's major shareholding was transferred from KLM to the Netherlands Antilles government.

The airline operates a network of regional scheduled services from Curacao to Caracas, Aruba, Bonaire, Georgetown, Grenada, Kingston, Paramaribo, Port of Spain, Port-au-Prince, Santa Domingo, St. Maarten and Valencia. Services also serve Atlanta, Georgia, and Miami, Florida, in the United States. The airline became a member of IATA in July 1990.

This government-owned airline commenced Douglas DC-9 twin-jet operations when it acquired three second-hand DC-9-15s from KLM. These were later replaced with new and second-hand DC-9-32s and in October 1982 ALM Antillean Airlines added two factory-new MD-82s, with a third leased from Continental Airlines in April 1988.

With over 800 employees and headquarters located at Hato International Airport, Curacao, the ALM fleet as of March 1992, included two de Havilland Dash 8-300s, three McDonnell Douglas MD-82s and one Lockheed L-188 Electra freighter.

The three DC-9-32 airliners used by ALM were as follows and all three are in airline service still. PJ-SNA c/n 47648 f/n 761 delivered to ALM on 16 January 1975, and today this DC-9-32 is in the United Kingdom operating as G-PKBM with British Midland. PJ-SNC c/n 47669 f/n 776 was delivered to ALM on 13 June 1975, and today is registered N932L with Trans-World Airlines. Finally, PJ-SNE c/n 47175 f/n 298 was initially delivered to Delta Air Lines on 28 April 1968, as N3334L before going to ALM. Today it is registered N3991C with Northwest Airlines carrying Fleet No. 9942.

Livery of the ALM fleet is colourful and highlighted by two broad fuselage bands of light blue and gold; these sweep from half-way down the fuselage to the tail unit where they narrow. The white tail unit carries six gold stars in a circle broken by the title 'ALM' at the base. The title 'ALM' is repeated on the forward fuselage — both being in light blue. The airliners' fuselage is off-white to wing level, being a very light grey lower surface. The engine nacelles are off-white and carry the inscription 'warmhearted wings' with the 'w' in gold and the rest in light blue. The registration of the airliner is positioned just above the windowline on the fuselage adjacent to the engine nacelles. Depicted is DC-9-32 PJ-SNA named *Aruba. (MDC)*

AMERICAN INTERNATIONAL AIRWAYS INC. (CKS)

United States of America

American International Airways is a division of Connie Kallita, undertaking cargo charters from its base at Willow Run Airport, Ypsilante, Michigan. The carrier was formed during 1972, and it received the necessary authorisation in 1984 to operate international charters. The present company title was adopted in December 1990.

It currently operates a fleet consisting of a wide variety of types which includes eight Douglas DC-8-50s, three DC-8-61s, six DC-8-63s, three DC-8-71s, one DC-8-73, and one Douglas DC-9-15F twin-engined aircraft. One Boeing 727-100, twelve Learjets and two Mitsubishi Mu-2s completes the fleet. A large number of the fleet are operated on lease, being acquired from such lease companies as Guinness Peat Aviation, United Aviation Services and General Air Cargo.

The single DC-9-15F operated by American International Airways is N9353 c/n 47154 f/n 201 ex-Mexican registered XA-BDM, originally delivered to Continental Airlines as a DC-9-15RC and registered N8912 on 28 November 1967.

The livery for American International Airways on their DC-9 airliners consists of an overall white aircraft with a red and blue pinstripe outlining the top and the bottom of the windowline, this extending from behind the cockpit to the rear of the fuselage. The all-white tail unit carries a styled arrowhead design in dark blue, this symbol being the airline logo. The aircraft registration in black is on the rear end of the fuselage under the tail. The airline title 'AMERICAN INTERNATIONAL AIRWAYS' together with the airline logo appears on the forward fuselage top in black or dark blue. The engine nacelles are white with a red and blue pinstripe.

Seen on the apron at Willow Run Airport is DC-9-33RC N94454 c/n 47291 f/n 343 delivered initially to Martinair Holland on 21 July 1968, as PH-MAN. On 1 November 1973 it was sold to Hawaiian Airlines as N94454 and during October 1978 it was leased to Itavia. Currently the airliner is on the inventory of Airborne Express and registered N933AX. *(MDC)*

ANSETT — ANA (AN/AAA)

Australia

Ansett Airlines was founded as Ansett Airways in February 1936 by a surface transport operator, Reginald M. Ansett. Forced to discontinue his omnibus service between Melbourne and Hamilton, Victoria, he joined the ranks of airline proprietors and bought a Fokker Universal and commenced a daily service over the same route on 17 February 1936, carrying air mail under contract from 25 May on. Purchasing a second aircraft, an Airspeed Envoy, he increased the service to twice daily in March 1937. Other routes were added so that by 1938 Ansett was serving Sydney, Adelaide and Broken Hill. A Lockheed Electra was the third aircraft, but unfortunately the complete fleet was destroyed by fire during 1939. During World War 2 Ansett was involved only in wartime military contracts. Commercial operations were resumed on 5 February 1945, over a small network linking Melbourne with Hamilton, Adelaide and Canberra. Later in 1945 it purchased three war-surplus DC-3s and extended the routes to Brisbane via Sydney and to Hobart. Being a very dynamic character, Reginald Ansett co-ordinated his many varied interests in the transport field by setting up a holding company, Ansett Transport Industries (ATI) on 31 May 1946, to control airline, busline, hotel, and truck-manufacturing aspects of the business.

On 8 October 1947 Barrier Reef Airways, founded by Ansett, began Consolidated Catalina flying-boat services to the island resorts off the Queensland coast near Mackay. In 1952 the operation of this subsidiary were consolidated with Ansett Airways. A year later the airline acquired the services and equipment of Trans-Ocean Airways, which on 24 February 1947, had started to operate Short Solent flying-boats from Sydney to Lord Howe Island and to Norfolk Island. During 1954 the Ansett fleet was consolidated into an efficient unit and the first of a fleet of Convair Cv.340s was delivered. In June 1957 Ansett made an offer of £A3 million for Australian National Airlines (ANA).

The world's airline fleet listing for May 1962 gave the Ansett Group as having on inventory thirty-three Douglas DC-3s, three DC-4 Skymasters, three Lockheed Electras, nine Vickers Viscounts, two Bristol 170s, and nine Fokker F.27 Friendships. As early as 1962 the Douglas sales team had attempted to interest Ansett in the DC-9-10 but its rather small capacity was considered unsuitable for Australian operations. However the airline placed a letter of intent with Long Beach for six of the larger DC-9-31s on 17 March 1964. The first aircraft VH-CZB c/n 47004 f/n 81 was delivered on 11 April 1967 and regular services on the east coast network commenced two days later. The new DC-9 soon took on an increased workload and began to appear on major routes throughout the Ansett system. By the time the final contracts had been fulfilled, the airline had a total of twelve DC-9s in service. The Ansett airliners had internal ventral airstairs to reduce reliance on ground services, low pressure tyres for secondary routes and airstrips and cockpit equipment enhancements. Withdrawal of the DC-9s commenced in 1981, the last Ansett commercial service being flown on 17 June 1982, from Launceston to Melbourne. All the Ansett DC-9s ended up in the USA, either with Midway Airlines or with the US Navy. VH-CZB became BuNo.162391: VH-CZA c/n 47003 f/n 86 BuNo.162390: VH-CZD c/n 47065 f/n 269 BuNo.162392: VH-CZF c/n 47325 f/n 515 BuNo.162393.

The DC-9s of Ansett-ANA had a most attractive livery which consisted of a white finish extending to just below the windowline, with the rest of the airliner light grey. A navy blue cheatline extended nose to tail below the windowline whilst a tapering red line was painted above the windowline. The red swept to join the all-red tail unit which was decorated by a very large 'A' outlined in white with 'ANSETT-ANA' in white at its base. The title was repeated in red on the fuselage top, whilst 'DC-9' in red and 'FAN JET' in dark blue appeared on the white engine nacelles. A red flash was painted on the forward fuselage, and the aircraft registration appeared in red at the rear of the fuselage.

Depicted is DC-9-31 VH-CZA c/n 47003 f/n 86 delivered on 17 March 1967, and now serving as a Skytrain II transport with the US Navy. It is seen on a pre-delivery flight over the coastline of southern California near Long Beach. (MDC)

ATI —
Aero Transporti Italiana (BM/ATI)

ATI (Aero Transporti Italiana Spa.) is Alitalia's wholly-owned subsidiary, and was formed on 13 December 1963, commencing domestic operations on 3 June 1964. It was formed to operate domestic services previously flown by Societal Aerea Mediterranea (SAM). In March 1985, Aermediterranea was incorporated into ATI, in which it had previously held a forty-five per cent stake.

Today the airline operates an extensive network of scheduled services within Italy and to the island of Sardinia. The company also undertakes group charter services between Italy, many European capitals and to North Africa. Headquarters for the airline is Naples and it currently employs some 2,000 personnel. It utilises a fleet of Douglas DC-9s and McDonnell Douglas MD-80 twin-jet airliners with frequent interchange of aircraft with the parent Alitalia.

The McDonnell Douglas aircraft inventory for 31 March 1992, listed ATI as having eight DC-9-32s and thirty-two MD-82 airliners on strength, however the fleet is now revised to seventeen and twelve. However with the close integration with Alitalia the maximum numbers of each type operated in any one year is quoted as twenty-six DC-9-32s and thirty MD-82s. Five of the DC-9s came from Aermediterranea when it merged with ATI during April 1985, and the DC-9-32 is configured to carry 123 passengers. The first DC-9-32 for ATI was I-ATIA c/n 47431 f/n 520 delivered on 24 July 1969. This airliner was originally intended for Alitalia to be registered I-DIZI but was not taken up.

Three of the ATI DC-9-32s carry names, these including I-RIKS c/n 47229 f/n 356 ex-I-DIKS *Basilcata*: I-RIZN c/n 47653 f/n 760 ex-I-ATJB *Riviera del Conero* : and I-RIZW c/n 47575 f/n 680 ex-I-ATIY *Lombardia*. The livery closely resembles that of Alitalia with a stylised 'A' logo in black with a light blue centre decorating the tail unit. The black is a continuation of the broad fuselage cheatline on the windowline. A large prominent title 'ATI' appears aft of the cockpit with the light blue centre again in the 'A'. The aircraft is white overall with natural metal engine nacelles with huge 'DC-9' imposed. The aircraft registration is in black, low on the fuselage just forward of the engine nacelles. The last two letters of the registration appear on the top of the tail unit, on the leading edge. Depicted is DC-9-32 I-RIKS. *(MAP)*

ATLANTIS AIRWAYS

Germany

Atlantis Airways was founded as Nordseeflug in Germany during 1966, commencing charter operations in mid-1968 and obtaining the necesary authority for trans-Atlantic flights in September 1968. European inclusive-tour (IT) and contract charters were undertaken with three new Douglas DC-9-32 twin-jet airliners which joined the fleet in 1970. These were D-ADIS c/n 47459 f/n 549 delivered on 15 January 1970: D-ADIT c/n 47450 f/n 535 delivered on 23 February 1970, and D-ADIU c/n 47457 f/n 620 delivered on 1 April 1970.

Based at Frankfurt, Atlantis Airways suspended activities late in 1972, and the three DC-9-32s were sold during January and March 1973.

The livery of Atlantis was most attractive with an all-white fuselage top, and a natural metal lower surface. A twin-colour line down the fuselage was dark red which covered the windowline and orange below. These colours extended to the tail unit with the red narrowing to cover the leading edge only, the orange covering the remainder of the tail. The airline emblem, a designed 'A' in white on a black circle was carried on the tail. The title 'ATLANTIS' appeared on the top forward fuselage, and the aircraft registration, preceded by the German national flag, appeared on the rear of the fuselage. The engine nacelles were natural metal, having 'DC-9' inscribed in black.

Depicted is DC-9-32 D-ADIS c/n 47459 f/n 549 delivered to Atlantis on 15 January 1970, seen on a pre-delivery test flight from the Long Beach factory in California. The airliner later became registered N942N. *(MDC)*

AUSTRIAN AIRLINES AG (OS/AVA)   Austria

Austrian Airlines (Osterreichische Luftverkehrs) was formed on 30 September 1957, involving a merger of two non-operating companies, Air Austria and Austrian Airways. The airline is now owned 51.9 per cent by the Austrian Government, ten per cent by Swissair, nine per cent by All Nippon Airways and one point five per cent by Air France. On 16 July 1989, Austrian inaugurated a twice-weekly joint service with Aeroflot and All Nippon Airways between Vienna and Tokyo via Moscow, utilising the Airbus A310-300s of Austrian. Other new routes added in 1989 were Vienna to Stuttgart, Nice and Lisbon, and Linz to Zürich and Düsseldorf. The airline also undertakes an extensive network of charter flights within Europe and Africa through its subsidiary Austrian Air Services which operates the Fokker 50.

The airline originally placed an order with Long Beach for nine Douglas DC-9-32s for delivery during 1971/72 and Austrian put the type into service on 22 June 1971, with a flight from Vienna to Frankfurt. Five DC-9-51s were ordered and this series was introduced into service on 7 September 1975, between Vienna and Munich, the airliner being OE-LDK *Graz* delivered on 25 August and had previously been registered with the Douglas Aircraft Company as N13627 for test flight purposes.

Livery for the Austrian Airline DC-9 fleet included a white overall airliner with the tail unit equally divided horizontally into three sections — two red and one white. The airline title 'AUSTRIAN' appeared in red on the forward fuselage top along with a red styled chevron aft of the cockpit. The engine nacelles were natural metal and the aircraft registration appeared in black at the extreme rear of the DC-9. During November 1979 Austrian leased one of its DC-9-32s OE-LDC c/n 47520 f/n 635 *Karnten* to Air Malta who applied their title. The airliner was returned to Austrian in April 1980. Another Austrian airliner DC-9-32 OE-LDG *Tirol* was c/n 47484 f/n 648 and was originally allocated as a DC-9-31 for Air West.

Depicted is DC-9-32 OE-LDA c/n 47521 f/n 629 delivered to Austrian Airlines on 10 June 1971 and named *Niederosterreich* and seen on a pre-delivery test flight from the Long Beach factory of the Douglas Aircraft Company. *(MDC)*

AVENSA (VE/AVE)

Venezuela

Aerovias Venezolonas (AVENSA) was founded on 13 May 1943, by an industrious group of Venezuelans, headed by an American, Henry Boulton. Air freight services commenced in December 1943, and passenger flights in May 1944, utilising a mixed fleet of aircraft which included three Ford Tri-Motors, a single Stinson Reliant and one Lockheed 12. In 1946 sufficient capital was raised to purchase a fleet of Douglas DC-3 airliners, and in 1953 twin-engined Convair Liners were added. The airline was initially primarily concerned with domestic services to the main cities in Venezuela, but in November 1954 embarked on international operations when the US Civil Aeronautics Board (CAB) granted AVENSA access to Miami via Jamaica, to which the New Orleans route was later added. In April 1976, the Venezuelan government's financial agency, Corporacion Venezolana de Fomento, purchased the thirty per cent stock held by Pan American since the foundation of the airline. The then international services of AVENSA and Linea Aeropostal Venezolana (LAV) were merged in 1961 to form Vias Internacionales Aereas (VIASA), in which AVENSA has a forty-five per cent holding. Today AVENSA is wholly-owned by the Venezuelan government.

Today the airline operates domestic scheduled passenger services from its base at Caracas to Barcelona, Cumana, Porlamor, Carupano, Puerto Ordaz, Maturin, Ciudad Bolivar, Aanaco, San Tome, Canaima, Borquisimeto, Coro, Las Piedras, Valera, Merida, San Antonio and Maracaibo. International services are operated to Mexico City and Panama City. The fleet consists of twelve Boeing 727-200s, three 727-100s, one 727-300, two Convair 580s, four Douglas DC-9-31s and three DC-9-51s. AVENSA commenced DC-9 twin-jet airliner operations early in 1967 when it acquired two new DC-9-14s from Long Beach — YV-C-AVM c/n 47056 f/n 89 and YV-C-AVR c/n 47060 f/n 109, these being joined by a new DC-9-32 YV-C-ACD c/n 47243 f/n 448 delivered on 27 February 1969.

In the mid-1970s the AVENSA fleet was supplemented with a further three leased DC-9-14/15s, as well as six more DC-9-32s purchased from Delta Air Lines between 1976 and 1978. For a while three DC-9-32s were operated in the United States by Midway Airlines on lease.

The original livery for the Avensa DC-9 fleet consisted of an all-white upper fuselage and natural metal lower, with a light blue windowline which extended from the cockpit to the rear of the fuselage. The all-white tail unit carried the airline winged motif in light blue, this including a map in white of South America. The leading and top edge of the tail unit was also blue, whilst the all-white engine nacelles were inscribed with 'DC-9' and had a blue symbol also. The AVENSA airline title appeared in black on the forward fuselage top, with the registration, also in black at the rear.

Depicted is DC-9-14 YV-C-AVR c/n 47060 f/n 109 delivered to the airline on 10 May 1967. It was later registered YV-57C. It is seen during a pre-delivery test flight from the factory at Long Beach. *(MDC)*

AVIACO (AO/AYC)　　　　　　　Spain

Aviaco (Aviacion y Commercio) the Spanish scheduled and charter carrier, was formed on 18 February 1948, as a private company by a group of Bilbao businessmen to operate all-cargo services. The idea was to utilise the scope for the generous freight load potential of the new Bristol Type 170 Freighter transport. During 1950 routes were opened within Spain, to the Balearic Islands and Marseille in France, plus to the nearby Spanish colonies in Africa. In 1953 Aviaco gained a five per cent interest in Royal Air Maroc.

Although full scheduled services were not introduced by the airline until 1987, by 1960 Aviaco was operating a Douglas DC-6 transport, six twin-engined Convair Liners, three Bristol Type 170 Freighters, and four small de Havilland aircraft. Today Aviaco conducts domestic operations in Spain with a fleet of twenty-three Douglas DC-9-30 twin-jet airliners and thirteen McDonnell Douglas MD-88 aircraft. These versatile airliners serve a wide network which includes services from Madrid to Almeria, Badajoz, Bilbao, Barcelona, Fuerteventura, Granada, Ibiza, Jerez, La Coruna, Lanzarote, Las Palmas, Menorca, Murcia, Mallorca, Malaga, Mahon, Oviedo, Pamplona, Palma, Reuis, Santander, San Sebastián, Seville, Tenerife, Vitoria, Valencia, Vigo, Valladolid and Zaragoza.

The 110-passenger DC-9-32s and DC-9-34s have been operated by Aviaco since June 1974. The first Douglas DC-9 for the airline was a DC-9-32 EC-CGN c/n 47637 f/n 731 delivered on 4 June 1974. In 1976 a number of DC-9-34CF aircraft were delivered to Aviaco. The airline also operates eight Fokker F-27-600 Friendship aircraft. Currently the Aviaco inventory includes fifteen DC-9-32s, four DC-9-34CFs and four DC-9-34 airliners.

Airline livery for Aviaco consists of a white upper surface, with a highly polished lower surface from the windowline. An attractive cheatline enveloping the windowline is dark and sky blue, this extending from the nose to the rear of the fuselage. The title 'AVIACO' is styled on the forward top fuselage with the 'A' enlarged. Forward of this is the Spanish national flag. The tail unit is white with a triangle design in dark blue. An orange band is at the top of the fin and below this the aircraft registration. The white engine nacelles have a company logo styled on the 'A'.

Depicted is DC-9-34CF EC-CTR c/n 47702 f/n 817 delivered on 30 April 1976, and seen during April 1982. Today this airliner is part of the Iberia fleet, still registered EC-CTR and it was once registered N19B. *(EMCS)*

BALAIR AG (BB/BBB/YBB)   Switzerland

Balair (Basler Luftverkehr) was formed during September 1925, commencing services in 1926 utilising a fleet of six Fokker F.VII/3m aircraft on routes to German cities in the Rhineland and to Lyons, France. Between 1925/30 Balair affiliated with D.L.H. (Deutsche Luft Hansa) on a joint operation on routes to and from Zürich to Berlin, Frankfurt and Munich. By 1931 the Balair fleet consisted of one Fokker F.VIIa and six Fokker F.VIIb/3ms. The airline was reformed during 1953, commencing new operations the same year with Swissair originally holding a thirty-six per cent interest, but this has since been increased to fifty-seven per cent. Today Balair operates passenger charters to destinations located in the Mediterranean, the Canary Islands, the Far East and the Caribbean. By March 1984 Balair was operating one Douglas DC-8-63F, one DC-10-30, two DC-9-30s and one McDonnell Douglas MD-80 twin-jet airliner. During 1985 an Airbus 310 was ordered, as of March 1992 the airline's inventory consisted of one Airbus A310-300, one Douglas DC-10-30, and three McDonnell Douglas MD-82s. Three more Airbus A310-300s are on order.

Switzerland's largest charter airline had at one time an all-Douglas twin-jet airliner fleet used on inclusive-tour and general charter flights to intra-European and North African destinations from the Swiss gateways of Basle, Geneva and Zürich. The first aircraft to join the Balair fleet from Long Beach was a DC-9-34 HB-IDT c/n 47712 f/n 815 delivered on 3 November 1976, and a DC-

9-51 was also operated on lease from the parent company, Swissair. However the historical archives reveal that a DC-9-33CF HB-IDN c/n 47465 f/n 584 was delivered on 17 April 1970, its last service being from Athens to Zürich on 31 October 1976. On 7 November 1976, it was returned to Long Beach before being re-registered N7465B. On 29 April 1977, it returned to Europe on lease to Itavia. By 7 November 1976, it had completed 12,852 flight hours, and 9,095 landings, and it eventually went into service with Swissair.

The Balair aircraft fleet is maintained by Swissair and flown by Swissair-trained pilots. The cockpit and entire technical equipment conforms to the high standards of Swissair and of the KSSU group which consists of KLM., SAS., and Swissair plus Union de Transports Aeriens (UTA). All aircraft are fitted with fully-automatic landing equipment to facilitate landing in the worst visibility.

Livery for the Balair fleet, up to March 1992 when it was changed, conforms to that used by Swissair. The colours of the Swiss national flag covered the tail unit, with 'BALAIR' in white at the base. A red cheatline covered the windowline with the aircraft registration in white at the rear of the fuselage. The top of the aircraft was white with the title 'BALAIR' aft of the cockpit, while the undersurface and engine nacelles were natural metal. Depicted is DC-9-33CF HB-IDN seen on a pre-delivery test flight from the Douglas factory at Long Beach. *(MDC)*

BONANZA AIR LINES
United States of America

Bonanza Air Lines, based in Las Vegas, Nevada, was initially a charter operator formed on 31 December 1945, in Phoenix, Arizona. It was certified on 15 June 1949, and operated its first service on 19 December 1949, to Reno, Las Vegas and Phoenix. It had previously operated inter-state charter services with effect from 5 August 1946, and used Douglas DC-3 airliners.

In 1966 the battle of the new jet airliners became very involved in the United States with the British-built BAC-111, the slightly larger Douglas DC-9 and the three-engined Boeing 727. Over the period of four years from 1966 every one of the many local carriers in the United States ordered jets, of which the majority were Douglas DC-9s.

The first local-service carrier to operate the new Douglas DC-9 twin-jet airliner was Bonanza Air Lines who introduced DC-9-11s on its main Phoenix to Las Vegas route on 1 March 1966. These aircraft were N945L c/n 45728 f/n 14 delivered on 19 December 1965, and N946L c/n 45729 f/n 16 delivered on 16 January 1966. The introduction of the Douglas DC-9 helped the airline to recover some valuable lost traffic. Later two DC-9-14s were added including N947L c/n 45730 f/n 37 delivered on 1 July 1966, which operated on Bonanza Air Lines' local routes and to west central Mexico.

During April 1968, a new airline called Air West was formed from the merger of Bonanza, West Coast and Pacific Airlines. From Bonanza the new airline inherited its DC-9s, and a Bonanza order with Long Beach for further airliners were delivered in Air West livery.

The Bonanza airline livery on the DC-9 was bright and attractive, dominated by the tail unit, this being rust-red with a large black 'B' imposed. The top part of the letter contained a sun image on white, and an airliner silhouette on white in the bottom portion. The fuselage was mainly all-white with a grey metal lower surface. Below the windowline a rust red cheatline topped by a black pinstripe ran the full length of the fuselage with the red merging with the colourful tail unit. The title 'BONANZA AIR LINES' in black appeared at the base of the tail, whilst 'BONANZA' in black was on the forward fuselage top. The engine nacelles were natural metal with the aircraft registration in black with a rust-red lightning flash on either side.

Depicted is DC-9-11 N945L c/n 45728 f/n 14 delivered to Bonanza on 19 December 1965. It is seen on a pre-delivery test flight from the factory at Long Beach over the lower slopes of the Sierra Nevada mountains. This DC-9 later went to Itavia as I-TIGA, later to Airborne Express as N925AX. *(MDC)*

BRITISH MIDLAND AIRWAYS (BD/BMA)

United Kingdom

British Midland can trace its origin back to 1938 and the formation of Air Schools. After World War 2 it entered the charter business and in 1949 formed Derby Aviation, which became Derby Airways in 1959, operating its first scheduled service on 18 July 1953. It operated a fleet of wartime Douglas DC-3 Dakotas. A further name change took place in 1964 when it became British Midland Airways, the company having moved its base from Burnaston to East Midlands airport in 1965.

During 1969 Minster Assets, an investment and banking group, acquired the airline; however, in 1978 directors of the company headed by Michael Bishop, affected one of the first management buy-outs when they purchased the company. In 1982, British Midland and Air UK formed Manx Airlines to operate schedule services from the Isle of Man. This was followed in 1983 by the purchase of Loganair from the Royal Bank of Scotland. Eurocity Express, later renamed London City Airways, was formed in 1987 to operate from the new London City Airport, this coming under the BMA banner in 1990. The airline has now pulled out of the airport. In March 1987 Airlines of Britain Holdings was formed to act as a holding company of BMA and its associates with Scandinavian Airlines System (SAS) having a 24.9 per cent stake.

On 18 June 1976, BMA signed a lease contract with the Douglas Aircraft Company for up to four DC-9-10 twin-jet airliners, and the first 90-seat airliner, an ex-Avensa DC-9-14 c/n 47056 f/n 89 was put into service on the London (Heathrow) to Tees-side route in September 1976. The first two DC-9s were flying under US registration, awaiting UK certification, this being granted in 1978. The current fleet consists of eight 100-seat DC-9-32s. Three ex-Austrian DC-9-32s were acquired in May 1990, these being G-ELDG *Orloff Diamond* ex-OE-LDG c/n 47484 f/n 648: G-ELDH ex OE-LDH c/n 47555 f/n 667: and G-ELDI *Regent Diamond* ex-OE-LDI c/n 47559 f/n 672.

British Midland operates a large network of scheduled services and is the second largest service operator from London (Heathrow). In 1991, BMA added three new international services to Palma, Nice and Malaga, to its route network from Heathrow, which today includes Amsterdam, Paris, Belfast, Birmingham, Brussels, Dublin, East Midlands, Edinburgh, Glasgow, Leeds/ Bradford and Tees-side. For many years BMA has been a major operator of scheduled services linking the Channel Islands with Belfast, Birmingham, East Midlands, Glasgow, Liverpool, Luton and Tees-side. On many of its services the high quality 'Diamond' service is offered and for many years BMA has been voted 'Best Domestic Airline' by the travel trade. Most of the Douglas DC-9 fleet are appropriately named to include 'Diamond.'

The British Midland DC-9 fleet has a very attractive livery consisting of a bright blue top to the airliner which also includes the tail unit and cockpit area. Below this a white pinstripe edge acts as divider from the grey lower surface which is also the colour of the engine nacelles. The initials 'BM' is inscribed in red on the tail and is repeated on the fuselage aft of the cockpit folllowed by 'British Midland' in white. A Union Jack appears on the nose, and the registration, in black, is placed on the fuselage just forward of the engine nacelles.

Depicted in landing sequence is the second DC-9 for the airline, a DC-9-32 G-BMAM c/n 47468 f/n 611 which was initially delivered to East African Airways as 5Y-ALR on 19 February 1971. Prior to UK certification the DC-9 was flown with the McDonnell Douglas US registration N504MD. The airliner is named *The Cullinan Diamond*. The first BMA DC-9 G-BMAK was a DC-9-32 c/n 47430 f/n 609 initially delivered to East African Airways as 5H-MOI on 9 December, 1970. It was flown by BMA as N503MD whilst awaiting certification and is named *The Stewart Diamond*. *(MAP)*

CARIBAIR

United States of America

Caribbean-Atlantic Airlines (Caribair) was incorporated in Puerto Rico by Dionisio Trijo on 27 February 1939, and on the first day of June took over the operations of Powelson Air Service, which had commenced flights between San Juan, the capital, and Ponce, the second largest city on the opposite side of the island during October 1938. Later that year, using ten-passenger Stinson aircraft, a route was opened to the Virgin Islands, another US possession in the Caribbean. A US Civil Aeronautics Board (CAB) certificate for these routes was obtained on 23 July 1942. In April 1945, more modern airliners were obtained, initially with the lease of Lockheed L.18 Lodestars from National Airlines, and a year later with the procurement of a fleet of Douglas DC-3s. On 27 December 1948, the Caribair network was expanded to include Ciudad Trajillo (Santa Domingo) in the Dominican Republic.

On 15 January 1958, a service was opened to St. Maarten in the Netherlands West Indies, and this route was extended to Guadeloupe in 1961. By this time, Caribair had added the Convair Cv.340 to its fleet of DC-3s. In order to utilise the short runway at St. Thomas, Virgin Islands, the Convairs were fitted with JATO which enabled them to clear the forbidding mountain top close to the climb-out path. Also in 1961, Trans-Caribbean Airways acquired a minority interest in Caribair, this being a logical move in support of its New York to San Juan trunk service. In December 1965, the airline converted its Convair Cv.340s to Rolls-Royce Dart-powered Convair 640s.

Based at Isla Verde, Puerto Rico, Caribair acquired the first of three Douglas DC-9-31 twin-jet airliners on 12 December 1967, to supplement the Convairs on its extensive network of services throughout the Caribbean, including the Leeward and Windward Islands, Trinidad & Tobago, Dominica, the US Virgin Islands and to Miami, Florida.

However, by 1968, the spirit of Caribair in the Caribbean appeared to be on the wane. Competition was on the increase, and the route structure needed strengthening, yet Caribair lost its case to operate a non-stop route from San Juan to Miami. The airline, one of the most colourful of the United States territorials, seemed ready for a take-over bid. On 27 October 1970, an acquisition offer from Eastern Air Lines came as no surprise, and on 21 May 1971, the CAB recommended a straightforward merger and a combined route structure and the routes, properties and the three Douglas DC-9s cost Eastern $10.4 million. The Long Beach-produced airliners were intregrated into the Eastern fleet.

The handful of DC-9s operated by Caribair had a mainly white fuselage with the lower portion plain metal. The tail unit and the fuselage cheatline, the latter covering the windowline, were a light sea-green colour, with an airline logo on the tail unit enclosed in a white circle. The airline title 'CARIBAIR' appeared on the fuselage top in sea-green, and the engine nacelles were also this attractive colour with 'fiesta jet' inscribed in white. The aircraft registration was in black at the rear of the fuselage. A light yellow pinstripe with black edge was used to border the sea-green livery, and a US national flag appeared under the cockpit.

Depicted is DC-9-31 N939PR c/n 47120 f/n 209 delivered to Caribair on 12 December 1967, seen on a pre-delivery test flight over the Pacific ocean off the coastline near the Douglas factory at Long Beach. In May 1971 the DC-9 depicted was transferred to Eastern Air Lines, being re-registered N899OE. *(MDC)*

CONTINENTAL (CO/COA) United States of America

Continental Airlines, owned by the huge Texas Air Corporation and currently the fourth largest US carrier, was formed on 15 July 1934, when it commenced services as Varney Speed Lines. In May 1937, Varney purchased the Denver to Pueblo route from Wyoming Air Service and moved its headquarters to Denver, Colorado. The name Continental Airlines was adopted later the same year, and development continued for a number of years until 1955 when the award of the route from Chicago to Los Angeles via Kansas City and Denver marked the full transition to a mainland trunk carrier. During October 1981, Texas Air, parent company of Texas International Airlines, acquired a controlling interest in Continental and, on 31 October 1982, Continental and Texas International commenced operations as a single carrier under the Continental title.

An extensive network of scheduled passenger services covers eighty-two domestic and forty-two international destinations. Its employees number 43,000. Since December 1990, Continental has been under Chapter 11 bankruptcy protection, resulting in a restructuring plan covering the airline, its parent company and fifty-one subsidaries. It believes that it could leave Chapter 11 bankruptcy protection by July 1992.

The McDonnell Douglas aircraft inventory for 31 March 1992, indicates that Continental operates thirty-four Douglas DC-9s, sixty-six MD-80s, and seventeen DC-10s. In addition it also operates a large number of Airbus A300B4s, Boeing 747-100/200, 727-100/200, 737-100/200/300. The Douglas DC-9 twin-jet fleet comprises mainly the DC-9-32s with a small number of DC-9-31s. The airline in the past has also operated the Douglas DC-9-14/15 and all the early Long Beach-built airliners were taken into the huge fleet with the incorporation of Texas International in October 1982, and New York Air in February 1987. However Continental itself was an early DC-9 operator when it totalled replaced its propliner fleet with four DC-9-14s and nineteen convertible DC-9-15RCs commencing 4 March 1966. The DC-9-31/32 airliners operated today seat 108 passengers, which includes eight in first class configuration.

The Continental livery changed on some of its fleet late in 1991, but otherwise has remained basically the same since the original markings were introduced in 1968. The cheatline consists of three basic colours, gold, red and orange. The lower colours have blended giving an appearance of a solid cheatline. The title 'CONTINENTAL' appears in black on the cabin roof along with the US national flag plus the airline motif which is red. This motif also appears in black on the gold tail unit. The top of the fuselage and engine nacelles are white. Depicted is DC-9-32 N531TX c/n 45847 f/n 349 since re-registered N17531 which was originally delivered to Swissair as HB-IFM on 17 October 1968. It is still part of the Continental Airline's huge fleet. *(MAP)*

DELTA AIR LINES (DL/DAL)

United States of America

Delta Air Lines, the Atlanta-based US major airline was founded in 1924. It was the world's first commercial crop dusting company, commencing scheduled passenger services in June 1929 between Dallas, Texas, and Jackson, Mississippi, as Delta Air Service Inc. By the end of 1934 as Delta Air Corporation it was high on the list of US airlines expanding, with services into the states of Alabama, Georgia and South Carolina. On its merger with Chicago & Southern Air Lines on 1 May 1953, the airline became known as Delta C & S Air Lines for short. In 1972 it absorbed Northeast Airlines which dated back to 1933, and many years later, in April 1987, when Delta took over Western Airlines it became the the third largest carrier in the United States. It is currently serving thirty-three countries, and during 1991 added twenty-one of the routes operated by Pan American. In November 1991 it added a further seventeen more routes mainly into Europe, adding to those already operated from its six main hubs located at Atlanta, Cincinnati, Dallas/Fort Worth, Salt Lake City, Orlando and Los Angeles. Its routes within the USA serve around 180 locations.

In April 1963, the Douglas Aircraft Company entered the medium-haul twin-jet field with the DC-9 prompted by Delta who immediately placed an order for fifteen aircraft, with an option for a similar number. It was Delta who inaugurated the world's first commercial DC-9 service when a DC-9-14 operated on the Atlanta-Memphis-Kansas City round trip on 8 December 1965, having commenced route-proving with the type on 29 November. From its launch order of fifteen DC-9-14s, Delta took delivery of fourteen before changing to the larger DC-9-32 effective from April 1967, eventually acquiring sixty-three new from Long Beach and acquiring a further fourteen more from its take-over of Northeast Airlines in August 1972. By the end of 1973, Delta completed a multi-million dollar refit programme, installing smoke emission devices on all its DC-9 fleet to reduce environmental pollution.

By the end of 1991 the large Delta DC-9 fleet alone had logged over four million landings. Currently the airline has on inventory many DC-9-32s which support the large fleet of over 100 MD-88 twin-jet airliners with more yet to be delivered. Delta had the distinction of taking delivery of the second and third DC-9-14 aircraft. It took delivery of its first DC-9-32 N3315L c/n 45710 f/n 100 on 9 April 1967.

The company name Delta is not only highly respected in the world's airline business, but is unique in that it was originally taken from the Mississippi Delta and is illustrated on all company material by a large dark blue and smaller red delta symbol. This is carried on the tail unit of the Delta aircraft fleet, and on the fuselage behind the cockpit and on the engine nacelles. This scheme is known as the 'widget'. The tail unit's blue delta has the 'DELTA' title in white, this being repeated on the mainly all-white fuselage, and below the delta symbol on the engine nacelles. Extending along the fuselage is dark blue cheatline at window level supporting a thin red pinstripe. The blue merges with the anti-dazzle panel on the nose. Depicted is DC-9-32 N1267L c/n 47262 f/n 412 delivered to Delta on 23 November 1968. (MAP)

EASTERN AIR LINES (EA/EAL)

United States of America

Eastern Air Lines was formed in 1926 as Pitcairn Aviation, commencing an air mail service between New York and Atlanta, Georgia during May 1928. In 1929 the company was acquired by North American Aviation, the name being changed to Eastern Air Transport. During 1938 North American relinquished its holding and the company adopted the EAL title after some reorganisation. Over the years several other airlines were absorbed, including New York Airways in 1931: Ludington Airlines in 1933: Colonial Airlines in 1956: Mackey Airlines in 1967, and Caribair in 1974. During 1982 the airline began operations on former Braniff routes to South America, serving Panama City, Barranquillo, Bogota, Cali, Quito, Guayoquil, Lima, La Paz, Ascension, Santiago and Buenos Aires. More than 100 points in thirty-four states in the USA, Canada, Mexico, the Bahamas and the Caribbean were served.

In 1934 Eastern was operating Curtiss Condors between New York and Miami once a day taking just over twelve hours with eight stops. Later in that year Douglas DC-2 airliners cut the journey to only three stops, whilst a nonstop service with Douglas DC-3s began on 16 January 1937, and in March 1940 Douglas DSTs were introduced on a sleeper service between New York and Houston. By March 1941 the airline was scheduling six daily flights from New York on the 1,100-mile route to Miami. The Air-Shuttle between New York, Washington and Boston was inaugurated by Eastern in 1961.

Eastern Air Lines became one of the earliest Douglas DC-9 operators when it took delivery of the first of an order for fifteen DC-9-14s on 26 April 1966. This was N8901E c/n 45742 f/n 26. These were soon joined by the larger DC-9-31, introduced on the Air-Shuttle on 1 February 1967. In February 1965, Eastern had placed its first order with Douglas at Long Beach for thirty-one aircraft and subsequent orders brought the DC-9-31 fleet to seventy-two airliners. Nine DC-9-51s were purchased in June 1976 and these, added to second-hand acquisitions, brought the number to twenty-five of the large DC-9 Series, thirty-eight 99-passenger DC-9-31s and twenty-five 120-seat DC-9-51s which remained in service until 1990. In Eastern service, EAL DC-9s accumulated some 4.5 million landings.

In its final days of operations Eastern was a subsidiary of the Texas Air Corporation, having suffered severe financial difficulties, compounded by a flight crew and an engineering strike during 1989, and subsequently the airline ceased operations on 18 January 1991.

The Eastern livery consisted of a complete natural metal finish on some of the fleet, including the DC-9, this being part of a huge fuel-saving programme by the airline. A cheatline of light and dark blue extended along the fuselage with the light blue on the windowline, before sweeping up the centre of the tail unit. The dark blue covered the nose, and on the fuselage top the US national flag was followed by the airline logo and then the title 'EASTERN' in blue outlined in white. The aircraft registration appeared in white on the fuselage on the dark blue cheatline just forward of the engine nacelles.

Depicted is DC-9-51 N991EA c/n 47728 f/n 858 delivered on 13 July 1977. It was later re-registered N409EA, and is seen on a pre-delivery test flight over the beautiful Sierra Nevada mountains inland from Long Beach. *(MDC)*

EMERALD AIRLINES (OD/EFF)

United States of America

Emerald Airlines, trading as Emerald Air, is a United States privately-owned regional carrier based in Austin, Texas, being formed in 1976, and has provided scheduled cargo services under contract since. These were fed into Purolator Courier's hub at Columbus, Ohio, another Douglas DC-9 operator. In June 1981, scheduled passenger services were inaugurated to feed into Pan America's run at Houston, Texas, from pick-up points throughout the state. During 1985 it was rumoured that the airline had ceased operations and filed for Chapter 11 protection under the United States bankruptcy code. However flight operations continued with contract charter flights to Atlantic City and several points in the Caribbean for casino vists, tours and involvement with contracts with the US Post Office.

Initial aircraft in the fleet included four DC-9-10F twin-jet freighters and a single Fairchild FH-227B. By 1991 the fleet consisted of five ninety-passenger DC-9-14s plus a similar number of DC-9-15RC aircraft, these being reduced to four DC-9-14s and two DC-9-15RCs by March 1992. The latest news is that Emerald Airlines has been merged into the new Braniff International based at Fort Worth, Texas, which operates the veteran DC-9-14 N931EA c/n 45698 f/n 5 ex EC-DIR of Spantax and leased from International Air Lease.

According to the McDonnell Douglas records Emerald Air today operates the veteran Douglas DC-9 c/n 45695 f/n 1 in its fleet, Emerald being the fifth owner; previous owners including Delta and Northwest Airlines. This twin-jet airliner has exceeded over 60,000 flight hours and 70,000 landings.

Over the past few years Emerald Air has adopted a new very smart livery with the main portion of the DC-9 being white with light grey undersurface. Under the windowline a series of thin dark green pinstripes extend to the rear of the fuselage from the nose and include the lower portion of the engine nacelles. The tail unit is dark green except for the leading edge which is white. The title 'Emerald Air' appears on top of the fuselage forward, with a new bird-like airline logo aft of the forward passenger door. The aircraft registration in white appears on the dark green portion of the engine nacelles. A dark green broad stripe appears on the undersurface of the forward fuselage.

Emerald Air did operate two DC-9-15RC aircraft ex-Air Florida, these being still in service in Italy with Unifly Express. The fleet today consists of four DC-9-14s which include N38641 c/n 47060 f/n 109 ex-YV-57C: N930EA c/n 45730 f/n 37 ex-OH-LYG: N931EA c/n 45698 f/n 5 ex-EC-DIR, and N932EA c/n 45699 f/n 8 ex-EC-GGZ. Depicted is N930EA. *(MAP)*

EUROFLY S.P.A. (EEU/Z6R)   Italy

Eurofly was established on 26 May 1989, as a Turin-based carrier operating inclusive tour (IT) charters to European, African and Middle East destinations. Operations commenced early in 1990 with two ex-Inex Adria Airways Douglas DC-9-51 twin-jet airliners. Apparently the company was formed as early as September 1978, to fulfil the transport needs of leading Italian industrial groups, headquartered in Turin. Shortly afterwards, executive services were added.

The airline has applied for routes linking Turin with Munich and linking Milan with Dreda. Alitalia and Olivetti-Eurofly each have a 45 per cent holding, the balance being held by San Paulo Finance.

A simple yet attractive livery is used by Eurofly with an overall white fuselage and an equally proportioned green and blue tail unit with green forward. The title 'eurofly' is positioned in blue below the windowline forward on the fuselage. The aircraft registration is above the windowline rear of the wing and the last two letters are repeated on the forward part of the tail. An Italian national flag is positioned aft of the registration on the fuselage. The engine nacelles are white with 'DC-9-51' and 'McDonnell Douglas' plus company emblem inscribed.

Douglas DC-9-51 I-FLYZ was delivered to Inex Adria as YU-AJP c/n 47697 f/n 816 on 19 May 1977, being previously registered N54UA. Up to 10 July 1984, this DC-9 had flown 18,752 hours and completed 14,951 landings. The second Eurofly DC-9-51 I-FLYY was delivered to Inex Adria as YU-AJU c/n 47754 f/n 856 also on 19 May 1977. It was previously registered N56UA. Depicted is I-FLYZ in landing configuration. *(MAP)*

EVERGREEN INTERNATIONAL AIRLINES (EV/EZ/EIA)

United States of America

Evergreen is an established US supplement cargo-carrier, today operating world-wide with services for the United Parcel Service (UPS) and the US Postal Service whilst International charters are undertaken. Until 28 November 1975 the company, which was taken over by Evergreen Helicopters of McMinnville, Oregon, was known as Johnson Flying Service, a company involved in supporting the US Forest Service on aircraft contracts and operating such veteran types as the Ford Tri-Motor, Douglas DC-2 and its ubiquitous successor the immortal Douglas DC-3. These were used to carry freight and fire-fighting equipment plus smoke jumpers as required in the suppression of forest fires.

The current Evergreen fleet consists of two Boeing 747-200 Combi, two Boeing 747-100F, five Boeing 747-100, two 727-200, four 727-100C, five 727-100F, one 727-100QC, one 727-100P, two McDonnell Douglas DC-8-73F, one DC-8-62F, two Douglas DC-9-32F, two DC-9-33F, two DC-9-33C and two DC-9-15F.

It was during 1976 that the first Douglas DC-9 twin-jet aircraft appeared in Evergreen livery, and since then a wide variety of the types have been operated successfully, these including the DC-9-DC-9-32CF, DC-9-33RC and the DC-9-15MC. Many of the DC-9s are still in service on scheduled flights between Texas and Mexico, and on US Air Force Logair military contracts. Currently

three of the DC-9s are in temporary storage at Marana Air Park, these being DC-9-15C N916F c/n 47044 f/n 165 ex-EC-EYS; N945F DC-9-33RC c/n 47194 f/n 324 ex-PH-DNP and N945 DC-9-33RC c/n 47279 f/n 337 ex-PH-DNR. Of the remaining five aircraft N915F DC-9-15C c/n 47061 f/n 207 is ex-XA-BCS; N932F DC-9-32F c/n 47355 f/n 452 is ex-I-DIKF, and N940F DC-9-33F c/n 47414 f/n 536 is ex-LN-RLW.

A natural metal finish has been adopted for the DC-9 fleet operated by Evergreen International, with an all-white tail unit which carries what appears to be a globe symbol with 'EVERGREEN' included. The title 'EVERGREEN INTERNATIONAL' is carried on the fuselage top along with the US national flag. A dark cheatline covers the windowline from nose to tail, with a similar broader cheatline just below. Aft of the cockpit is a six star circle symbol and the aircraft registration is carried on the natural metal engine nacelles.

Depicted is DC-9-33RC N933F fitted out as a freighter aircraft, c/n 47191 f/n 280 which was initially delivered to KLM as PH-DNM on 30 April 1968. It came to the USA and for a while was leased by International Air Lease to Aeroquetzal based in Guatemala but registered in the US as N33UA. This was prior to its purchase by Evergreen. *(MAP)*

FINNAIR (AY/FIN)

Finland

In Finland air transport was suspended in 1945 under the Allied Armistice Agreement. During 1946 the Finnish government acquired a seventy per cent interest in the pre-war airline Aero O/Y and the route to Stockholm was reopened on 1 November 1947, when permission to operate air services was granted. Nine Douglas DC-3 airliners were purchased and a new airline was gradually developed. On 15 April 1951, a service was operated to Düsseldorf and Hamburg, by which time the company was operating under the name Finnair.

The national airline of Finland has been operating products of the Douglas Aircraft Company since 1941, when Aero O/Y flew the DC-2 airliner. Today it operates the Douglas DC-10 and the McDonnell Douglas MD-80 series and the new MD-11. In the large fleet there are twelve 122-seat DC-9-51s and five 126-seat DC-9-41s operated on an all-economy layout. Finnair's first DC-9, a Series 14, was delivered on 24 January 1971, and in subsequent years the airline has operated nine DC-9-14/15s, one DC-9-15MC (Multiple Change) and seven DC-9-41s and eighteen DC-9-51s.

Today Finnair operates one of the world's densest domestic networks, relative to the population, serving a 22-point system. In all, some 34 destinations are served, mainly in Europe. Charter flights are also operated to more than 40 destinations, mainly to the popular holiday resorts on the Mediterranean, in the Canary Islands, plus resorts in south-east Asia.

Co-operative partners of Finnair are Japan Air System, the Scandinavian Airlines System (SAS), Swissair and what was known as Aeroflot. In April 1991, an agreement with Aeroflot was made to set up a joint venture company to develop international traffic from St. Petersburg, using western-built aircraft. Initially Douglas DC-9s would be operated. This venture should be complete and operating by 1993.

The national flag of Finland with its blue and white colours forms the basis of the Finnair livery. The fuselage is white to wing level, being grey underneath, whilst a broad blue cheatline extends the length of the fuselage at window level. The title 'FINNAIR' is in dark blue, leaning backwards slightly, and is on the top of the forward fuselage. The tail unit is decorated with the blue cross flag of Finland. The engine nacelles are decorated with white panels, and the aircraft registration is on the upper fuselage in dark blue, positioned just forward of the engine nacelle. Depicted is DC-9-51 OH-LYN c/n 47694 f/n 805 delivered to the airline on 23 January 1976, and seen during a pre-delivery test flight from Long Beach. It is still in service with Finnair and up to 22 July 1984, had flown 19,986 hours and accomplished 17,311 landings. *(MDC)*

GARUDA (GA/GIA)   Indonesia

Garuda Indonesia, formerly known as Garuda Indonesian Airways, the state-owned Indonesian national airline, was formed on 31 March 1950, by the Indonesian government and KLM, as the successor to the post-war Inter-Island Division of KLM and the pre-war KNILM.

When KLM opened up its route to Curacao it achieved its pre-war ambition to link the West Indies network with the home country. In the East Indies political differences led to the abandonment of the route network of the subsidiary KNILM which had been operated since World War 2 by a squadron of the Dutch Air Force operating a fleet of Douglas DC-3 transports. On 1 August 1947, KNILM's services were absorbed by KLM, but problems arose when the connecting link was threatened by an embargo from India on KLM flights. This was applied on 4 August 1947, but its circumvention by use of a route through Ceylon led to its cancellation on 7 October. After a very disorganised period whilst Indonesia was emerging as an independent nation, KNILM became Garuda Indonesian Airways in December 1949, owned jointly by the Indonesian government and KLM. In due course, on 12 July 1954, the government exercised its rights to buying KLM's shareholding, and in September 1956 even the technical collaboration with KLM ceased, ending rather sadly a story of brilliant achievement. Most of Garuda's main services were provided by a fleet of Convair 240 airliners. Later Lockheed Electras were acquired to bring the Indonesian airline up-to-date and give it the ability to meet on more equal terms the many modern jet airliners passing over its home territory.

On 1 January 1963, Garuda took over De Kkroonduif's domestic operations in West New Guinea, but a year later these were handed over to PT Merpati Nasontara, the nationalised domestic operator.

In October 1978 Garuda took them over. The other aviation-related subsidiaries of Garuda include Sanur Beach and the catering subsidiary PT Angkasa Atra Sarona and Sdtriavi Travel Service.

Over a ten year period between October 1969 and August 1979, the airline acquired a total of twenty-five new Douglas DC-9-32s of which eighteen remain in service today. The 97-seat DC-9-32s are fitted out in a configuration which includes twenty first-class and seventy-seven economy, and are utilised mainly on its extensive domestic network, linking no less than thirty-five of the main cities located throughout the archipelago. This domestic network extends one tenth of the way round the world from the Jakarta base.

Plans are in hand apparently to transfer all domestic operations to its wholly-owned subsidiary, Merpati Nusantara, and already two DC-9-32s PK-GNF c/n 47569 f/n 683 and PK-GNR c/n 47744 f/n 837 have been transferred. A further seven are to follow while the remaining DC-9s are expected to be replaced by Boeing 737s. The airline also operates the Douglas DC-10 and the MD-11.

The current Garuda livery was unveiled during September 1985, being designed by Walter Londor & Associates of San Francisco. The dramatic new image centres on a bird motif, made up of five stripes to represent the five national ideals, the stripes appearing in various shades of light-blue and turquoise which gets progessively greener. The bird motif is displayed on an all-dark blue fin and also appears alongside the 'Garuda Indonesia' title on an overall white fuselage. An Indonesian national flag appears alongside the forward passenger door. The aircraft registration is positioned on the fuselage by the all-white engine nacelles. Depicted is PK-GNM c/n 47701 f/n 822. *(MAP)*

GERMANAIR

Germany

Germanair was a Frankfurt-based charter airline which commenced operations with Douglas DC-6B aircraft during 1965. On 28 April 1969, it took delivery of a single Douglas DC-9-15 twin-jet airliner registered D-AMOR c/n 45787 f/n 127 which it utilised on inclusive-tour (IT) flights to the popular island holiday resorts in the Mediterranean, to North Africa and the Middle East. The DC-9 was operated until 27 August 1969, when it was replaced by BAC One-Eleven airliners.

The Germanair DC-9-15 had a very varied career having been initially delivered to Swissair as HB-IFE on 26 June 1967, and after service with Germanair went to Kenya Airlines as 5Y-AKX and then to South Korea as HL-7205. After each change of ownership it returned to the USA and so on four occasions was registered

N1793U. This was applied after its service in South Korea after which it remained in the United States registered N9348.

The single Germanair DC-9-15 is seen on a pre-delivery test flight over the Sierra Nevada mountains in California, near the Long Beach factory of the Douglas Aircraft Company. The airliner had an all-white top and natural metal lower fuselage. A crimson red cheatline on the windowline went from nose to tail on the fuselage. The forward portion of the tail unit was red with a styled German eagle design in white on black. The engine nacelles were natural metal with 'DC-9' imposed, and the top of the fuselage had the German national flag and the aircraft registration in black near the tail and the airline title 'GERMANAIR' in black on the forward fuselage top. (MDC)

GHANA AIRWAYS (GA/GHA)　　　Ghana

Ghana Airways was formed on 4 July 1958, by the Ghananian government when the former West African Airways Corporation began to prepare for the division of the company. Ghana, previously the Gold Coast, was representing a new country which led the field and which saw itself as the prime mover in a country growing in the number of individual airlines. Trunk services commenced on 16 July 1958, under British Overseas Airways Corporation supervision, and a domestic pattern was taken over from WAAC on 1 October. Early in 1959 a number of de Havilland Heron aircraft were delivered for these services. Since 14 February 1961, Ghana Airways has been wholly government-owned.

The airline's fleet today includes a single Douglas DC-10-30 and a single DC-9-51 9G-ACM c/n 47755 f/n 878 delivered from Long Beach, California, brand-new on 13 July 1978. It is fitted out for ten first-class and 122 economy-class passengers. It shares both the regional and domestic services with a Fokker F-28-2000 Fellowship, linking Accra with Abidjan, Banjeel, Canakry, Cotonou, Dakar, Freetown, Lome, Monravia, Las Palmas and Takoradi. Currently the airline is looking to replace the DC-9-51 with the later, larger capacity twin-jet MD-82 airliner.

Prominent in the Ghana Airways livery is the Ghananian national colours of red, yellow and green, incorporating within the motif, the national black five-pointed star. This appears on the tail unit of the DC-9-51. The airliner is white overall with the 'GHANA AIRWAYS' title on the top of the forward fuselage in black together with the national flag of Ghana. The aircraft registration is on the all-white engine nacelles. Depicted is 9G-ACM seen on a pre-delivery test flight from the Long Beach factory prior to delivery. *(MDC)*

GREAT AMERICAN AIRWAYS (FD/GRA/ZGM)

United States of America

Great America Airways commenced operating as a certificated US airline with worldwide charter authority during 1979, and today operates passenger charter services throughout the United States, Mexico and Canada. Based at Reno, Nevada, the airline made its first ever revenue flight on 26 September 1979, between Reno and Seattle using DC-9-15 N1068T c/n 45782 f/n 114 a Douglas twin-jet airliner initially delivered to TWA on 30 May 1967. The Long Beach-built airliner was configured for the maximum of ninety passengers.

The airline is involved in group charter and contract jet flights from and to Reno and Lake Tahoe resorts and the area casinos from points spread throughout the western United States and British Columbia in Canada. A second DC-9-15 has been added

this being N1070T c/n 45784 f/n 140 which was initially delivered to TWA on 19 August 1967.

Livery for Great American Airways consists of white top and polished metal undersurface. The white extends to just above wing level with a red cheatline enveloping the windowline and commencing narrow and broadening towards the rear fuselage. The title 'Great American Airways' is on top of the forward fuselage with American in red, the rest being black. A company logo decorates the white tail unit, this appearing to be 'BM' in a broken black circle. The registration is in black on the base of the tail unit and the engine nacelles are polished metal. Depicted is N1068T seen parked at Reno, Nevada. *(EMCS/John Kimberley)*

HAWAIIAN AIR (HA/HAL)   United States of America

Hawaiian Airlines was founded by the local steamship company as early as 30 January 1929, when it was known as Inter-Island Airways. It opened its service with two Sikorsky S.38 amphibians linking the outer islands of Hawaii with Honolulu on 11 November 1929. In 1934 air mail contracts were obtained and during the following years the fleet was augmented by the larger Sikorsky S.39 amphibian. The Civil Aeronautics Board awarded a permanent route certificate on 16 June 1939, and it was on 1 October 1941 that the airline assumed its present name. In that year three Douglas DC-3 airliners were obtained and on 20 March 1942 an inter-island freight service was started, this fulfilling a genuine need in transporting perishable foods.

Hawaiian held a monopoly on air services in the islands until 6 June 1949, when Trans-Pacific Airlines (later changed to Aloha Airlines) began scheduled services in direct competition. On 29 November 1948, the CAB finally authorised scheduled services to TPA giving Hawaii the benefits of a competitive service. The two airlines operated identical routes linking the islands and on 23 December 1965, Hawaiian introduced Dart-powered Convair twin-engined airliners with the successful Douglas DC-9 twin-jet airliner being introduced in March 1966.

Currently Hawaiian Airlines operates scheduled passenger services linking the islands of Lihue, Kauai: Kahului, Maui; Kapulua, West Maui; Hoolehua, Molokai: Lonai: Kona and Hilo, Hawaii.

Jet services commenced in 1 April 1966, with the introduction of two 85-passenger Douglas DC-9-15s N901H c/n 45724 f/n 20 and N902H c/n 45724 f/n 22, these airliners being so popular that in September the purchase of two larger DC-9-31s was announced. These were delivered in 1967/68 being N903H c/n 47149 f/n 202 delivered on 22 November 1966, and N905H c/n 47150 f/n 284 delivered on 5 April 1968. This eventually led the airline to operate a large fleet of the Long Beach-built twin-jet airliners. Today the Hawaiian fleet includes no less than thirteen DC-9-51 aircraft, plus a small number of MD-81s.

These very popular aircraft are utilised on a very high-frequency or multiple daily inter-island flights serving seven airports on six islands in the Hawaiian group. The airline livery is attractive with an overall white finish with a red flower and a Hawaiian 'hula hula' girl's portrait imposed. This takes up most of the tail unit. A broad double sash of red and purple envelops the mid-fuselage, this sweeping to the rear of the fuselage top with the flower and maiden's head in front. 'HAWAIIAN AIR' appears on the white engine nacelles and the registration, like the titles, is in red and on the fuselage at the rear. Depicted is N699HA c/n 47763 f/n 879 DC-9-51 delivered on 11 July 1978, and still in service today. It is seen on a pre-delivery test flight from the Long Beach factory in California. *(MDC)*

HUGHES AIR WEST

United States of America

Hughes Air West was established on 3 April 1970, when the huge Hughes Air Corporation, headed by one of the most enigmatic personalities that the world of air transport, or indeed any other industry, has ever encountered, Howard Hughes; bought the assets of Air West. Hughes, heir to a large fortune which his father amassed in the Hughes Tool Company, was a famous record-breaking pilot during the 1930s. In 1937 he bought eighty-seven per cent of the TWA stock and controlled the airline's fortunes with spectacular success for more than thirty years. Forced to surrender absolute control in 1960 he eventually sold his TWA stock for $566 million in 1966. Howard Hughes kept in practice as it were, by taking over the merged local service airline, Air West, on 21 July 1969. Hughes' association, to the extent of adding his name officially to the airline — Hughes Air West — was perhaps the portent of dramatic revival.

Hughes Air West became a major carrier which served more than fifty cities in the western United States, Mexico and Canada. The largest proportion of its 'Sundance' fleet was made up of Douglas DC-9 twin-jet airliners and included twenty-nine 103-passenger DC-9-30s and ten seventy-five seat DC-9-10s. The majority of these were taken over from Air West and the others were purchased mostly from Eastern Airlines, Continental Airlines, and Hawaiian Airlines in the mid-1970s. With effect from 1 October 1978, Hughes Air West offered a new 'business coach' section featuring four-abreast seating on all its DC-9s. These airliners were unique in having closed overhead storage compartments, whilst the range and payload capabilities were boosted through a programme of upgrading the engines on its fleet of DC-9s.

The airline also operated a fleet of Fairchild Hiller FH-227 prop-jet airliners, these being required on feeder routes and for getting into the smaller airports on its routes, one such airport being Coos Bay/Northbend in Oregon. Passengers from San Francisco flew Hughes Air West DC-9 to Crescent City on the Californian/Oregon border, then transferred to a FH-277 to fly to Coos Bay. The complete Hughes Air West fleet was known in some circles as 'Hughes Yellow Bellies' due to the bright yellow finish. On 1 October 1980, the airline was acquired by Republic Airlines, and today some of the ex-Hughes Air West DC-9-31s are still operating in Northwest livery, this being the airline who took over Republic.

Easily distinguished by their overall canary-yellow finish, the Hughes Air West fleet were a common sight at most airports, large and small, on the Pacific coastline. The title 'HUGHES AIR WEST' was styled in blue low on the forward fuselage. A three-image airline logo appeared on the tail unit in blue, and the aircraft registration appeared in blue on the yellow engine nacelles of the DC-9 fleet.

Depicted is DC-9-31 N9335 c/n 47337 f/n 415 delivered to Air West on 27 November 1968, and subsequently transferred to Hughes Air West. It is seen at Crescent City, California, on 18 August 1971. Note the airstair, most convenient at small airports served by the airline. *(A. Pearcy)*

IBERIA —
Lineas Aereas de España (IB/IBE)

Spain

Iberia is the national airline of Spain founded in 1927 as Lineas Aereas de España, from a succession of carriers dating back to 1921. After World War 2 the airline was re-established, opening services first to London on 3 May 1946, and to Rome the following August. With most of the main cities in Spain still an arduous journey by any form of surface transport, a domestic network was a necessary part of Iberia's planning and for some years after World War 2 a fleet of Junkers Ju.52/3m Tri-Motor airliners were used.

The airline is state-owned and is controlled through the Instituto Nacional de Industria who hold 99.7 per cent. However, during 1990 the airline was substantially re-organised to create a number of clearly-defined profit centres, thus clearing the way for privatisation. The carrier has established subsidiary airlines Binter Canarias and Binter Mediterraneo to operate scheduled passenger services in the Canary Islands and Balearic Islands, Eastern Levante, France, Italy and North Africa respectively. Binter Cantabria is planned to provide local services in northern Spain and link with points in France. Iberia is also a major shareholder of 48 per cent in Viva Air, a charter carrier owned jointly with Lufthansa. Cargo Sur operates all-cargo scheduled services, and Iberia is one of the five partner airlines in the Atlas aircraft maintenance group.

Iberia uses the Douglas DC-9 on its intra-European routes, the first aircraft, a DC-9-32 EC-BIG c/n 47037 f/n 121 joining the fleet on 30 June 1967, and still in service. A total of thirty-five DC-9 twin-jet airliners were purchased direct from the Douglas Aircraft Company at Long Beach, consisting of thirty-one DC-9-32s and four DC-9-33RC (Rapid Change) airliners. Today the Iberia fleet consists of eighteen DC-9-32s.

The regal livery of Iberia vividly combines the colours of the Spanish national flag giving an easy clue to the well-known holiday attraction of Spain. Triple cheatline in red, orange and yellow commence aft of the cockpit roof, sweeping along the all-white fuselage bordering on the windowline. An 'IB' tail motif in red and yellow appears on the tail unit, while the 'IBERIA' title in white is carried on the fuselage on the red portion of the triple coloured cheatline. The aircraft registration is duplicated, one appearing forward on the tail and the other at wing level on the rear fuselage by the engine nacelles which are white. The registration has a Spanish national flag emblem positioned in front of it.

Depicted is DC-9-32 EC-BIM c/n 47088 f/n 108 delivered to Iberia on 28 October 1967, and named *Ciudad de Santander*. This veteran airliner is still in active service today with the company. *(MAP)*

Intercontinental de Aviacion (RS/ARP)

Colombia

Formed in 1965 Intercontinental de Aviacion was known until December 1982, as Aeropesca Colombia (Aerovias de la Pesca y Colonizacion del Swoeste Colombiano) and is privately-owned. It provides scheduled domestic passenger and cargo services linking its headquarters located at Bogota with Arauca, Cali, Cucuta, Florencia, Ipiales, Leticia, Medelin, Pereira, Popayan, Riohacha, San Andres, Santa Marta, Tumaco, Valle and Valledupar. Further routes are planned linking Bogota to Cucata and Maracaibo, and with Cali to Tulcan and Pasto. General cargo and specialised livestock are also undertaken.

In October 1982, the airline acquired two Douglas DC-9-15 twin-jet airliners on lease to supplement its Vickers 828 Viscount airliners. Today the DC-9 fleet has been increased to four, assisted by a single Viscount 828, which is in storage, and a single Curtiss C-46F Commando freighter. The four DC-9-15s are fitted out for eight-five single-class passengers and two are on lease from Guinness Peat Aviation.

The four DC-9-15 aircraft are HK-2864X c/n 45721 f/n 44 originally delivered to KLM on 17 August 1966 as PH-DND last registered N908DC: HK-2865X c/n 45722 f/n 55 another KLM aircraft ex-PH-DNE ex-N2896W and now named *Ciudad de Popayan*: HK-3486X c/n 47125 f/n 388 delivered originally as XA-SOG to Aeronaves de Mexico on 7 October 1968, and finally HK-3564X c/n 47127 f/n 417 ex-XA-SOI also ex-Aeronaves de Mexico.

An unusual yet attractive livery has been adopted for the DC-9s operated by Intercontinental de Aviacion. The current livery was introduced during the early 1990s for the DC-9 fleet. A white top and natural metal lower surface to the fuselage was shared with a dull mustard-yellow and dark-blue cheatline, with a white dividing pinstripe. This cheatline broadened to sweep up the tail unit which has a white airline logo design plus the aircraft registration. The fuselage top has the title 'INTERCONTINENTAL' in dark-blue followed by 'Columbia' in a light print. The Colombian national flag appears below the cheatline adjacent the cockpit, and the engine nacelles are natural metal with 'DC-9' and the McDonnell Douglas name and company motif included.

Depicted is DC-9-15 HK-3486X c/n 47125 f/n 388 which is currently on lease from Guinness Peat Aviation. *(MAP)*

IPEC Aviation (IN/IPA)

Australia

IPEC Aviation was formed in 1976 to fly the Bass Strait freight service, linking Essendon Airport, Melbourne, with Launceston, Tasmania. The company is owned and is a division of Mayne Nickless and is called Interstate Parcel Express Company — IPEC. It also provides charter flights the length and breadth of Australia, with the parent company being one of the largest, specialising in fast freight and overnight services.

Services were initially inaugurated on 1 February 1982, utilising a single Armstrong-Whitworth Argosy freighter, this being replaced in June 1982 with an ex-Jugoslav-operated Douglas DC-9-33CF YU-AJP. A second similar DC-9 was added in November 1989, and this enabled the three A-W Argosies then in use, to be retired.

The versatile DC-9 twin-jet freighters today fly the Melbourne to Launceston route several times daily, and are also utilised on schedules to Adelaide, Sydney and Brisbane plus being engaged on general cargo work.

The Douglas DC-9-33RC VH-IPC c/n 47193 f/n 311 ex-PH-DNO of KLM arrived in Australia in November 1989 registered N941F, whilst VH-IPF DC-9-33CF c/n 47408 f/n 467 ex-YU-AJP of Inex Adria arrived in June 1982 as N936F. A simple livery identifies the IPEC DC-9s which have a yellow upper surface bordering below the windowline with a black pinstripe. The tail unit, except for the rudder, is also yellow and the 'IPEC' title appears on the tail unit and top of the fuselage. Lower half of the aircraft and engine nacelles are light grey, the registration being in black on the nacelles. Depicted is VH-IPC seen at Eagle Farm airport in September 1991. The DC-9 VH-IPC is named *Spirit of Enterprise* and VH-IPF is likewise named *Spirit of Endeavour*. (Bruce Potts)

JAC — Jugoslav Airlines (JU/JAT)   Jugoslavia

Jugosolevnski Aerotransport was formed in 1946. The pre-war Jugoslav airline Aeroput founded in Belgrade in 1927 went out of existence in May 1941, when the country was overrun by the German troops. A new company — JAT — was organised by the government to take over interim services, initially using military aircraft. The first aircraft type in operation during 1947 was Junkers Ju.52/3m transports, these soon being replaced by Douglas DC-3 aircraft.

Today the wholly state-owned airline operates on extensive scheduled passenger services on a network servicing nineteen domestic points and many cities in western Europe, Scandinavia, eastern Europe and the Middle East. Air Jugoslavia is a subsidiary formed to operate charters, using JAT equipment when required. The airline undertakes maintenance for its own aircraft and for other operators. The Jugoslavian carrier also operates Airlift, a tour operator, JAT Catering, JAT Training Centre, JAT Medical Centre, Agricultural Aviation, two airports and JAT ground transportation.

On 19 January 1970, JAT announced its first order with the Douglas Aircraft Company for five DC-9-32 twin-jet airliners, after having already provided DC-9 services on its European and Middle East routes since April 1969, using a DC-9 leased on an interim basis. In the configuration ordered by JAT, the airliner initially seated ninety-nine passengers, since changed to a twin-class 107-passenger layout. A total of sixteen DC-9s were eventually purchased, nine of which remain in service on both domestic and European routes. One DC-9-32 has been on lease to Air Djibouti since October 1986.

In the JAT livery the colours of the Jugoslav national flag are widely used. The current livery was introduced during August 1985 with delivery of the airline's first Boeing 737-300. With the DC-9-32 fleet it provides the basic blue and red of the cheatline with blue on the windowline with a red stripe below, all on an overall white fuselage. The titling is unique, featuring 'Yugoslav Airlines' on the starboard side in red, and 'Jugoslovenski Aerotransport' in blue on the port side. The red and white 'JAT' logo remains unchanged and is displayed boldly on the predominantely blue tail unit. A Jugoslav national flag appears on the base of the tail unit which is white, and the aircraft registration in red appears on the rear of the fuselage by the tail. The last two letters of the registration appear on the front of the fuselage at cockpit level. Engine nacelles appear to be natural metal with 'DC-9' and 'McDonnell Douglas' plus company motif inscribed.

Depicted is DC-9-32 YU-AHU c/n 47532 f/n 626 delivered on 7 May 1971, and still in current service with JAT. It was delivered via London (Heathrow) where it arrived on 9 May. (MAP)

KENYA AIRWAYS (KQ/KQA)   Kenya

Kenya Airways was formed on 22 January 1977, by the Kenyan Government to operate both domestic and international scheduled services from Kenya after East African Airways ceased operations owing to severe financial problems. Three DC-9-32 twin-jet airliners were transferred to Kenya Airways upon its formation. Scheduled passenger services began early in February 1977 linking Nairobi with Cairo, Athens, Rome, London, Frankfurt, Paris, Khartoum, Dubai, Jeddah, Bombay, Addis Ababa, Mogadishu, Seychelles, Entebbe, Harare, Dar-es-Salaam and Lusaka. Internal services operated from Nairobi to Mombasa, Malindi and Kisumu. Kenya Flamingo Airways was the carrier's charter subsidiary, utilising aircraft from the parent company. The Kenya Airways fleet listing for March 1985 gave the airline as operating three Boeing 707-320Bs, one -720B, one Douglas DC-9-30 and two Fokker F.27-200 Friendships.

Until economic and political problems grounded East African Airways Corporation on 1 February 1977, it had served as the national airline of Kenya, Uganda and Tanzania. The EAAC fleet included three Douglas DC-9-32 airliners, these being 5H-MOI c/n 47430 f/n 609 delivered on 9 December 1970 and registered in

Tanzania; 5Y-ALR c/n 47468 f/n 611 delivered on 19 February 1971, and registered in Kenya, and 5X-UVY c/n 47478 f/n 612 delivered on 24 February 1971 and registered in Uganda. One Kenya Airways DC-9 was leased to Air Tanzania until October 1977, but upon its return to Kenya was disposed of with another DC-9. Kenya Airways retained the remaining DC-9-32 5X-UVY until 1989. It was fitted out for twelve first class and eighty-five economy class passengers.

The Kenya Airways DC-9 airliners had a white top and tail unit with a natural metal lower surface. A dark red cheatline extended from nose to tail covering the windowline, this having a white border with a pinstripe. The title 'KENYA AIRWAYS' and the Kenya national flag appeared on the forward fuselage top. Engine nacelles were natural metal with 'DC-9' and the McDonnell Douglas name and logo inscribed. The aircraft registration appeared in black at the base of the tail unit.

Depicted is DC-9-32 5X-UVY registered in Uganda having c/n 47478 f/n 612. The archives reveal that this airliner was eventually registered in Kenya as 5Y-BBR. It was later sold in the USA and registered N942ML with the now defunct Midway Airlines. *(MAP)*

LINEA AEROPOSTAL
VENEZOLANA (LV/LAV)

Venezuela

Linea Aeropostal Venezolana (LAV) can trace its history back to 1929 when the French Aeropostal company failed to achieve its ambition of linking France and the Caribbean via Natal, French Guiana, and Venezuela. At the same time as the formation of Air France and the dissolution of Aeropostale, the Venezuelan branch of the airline was bought by the Venezuelan government, which renamed it Linea Aeropostal Venezolana (LAV). At first the company formed part of the Ministry of Labour and Communications, but in 1937 it became an autonomous government-owned corporation. In 1938 its French-built Latecoere 28 airliners were replaced by Lockheed Electras and Lodestars. New capital was provided and the route network was extended. The following year the airliner headquarters were transferred from Maracay to Maiquetia, the airport serving Caracas, and the fleet was further modernised by the acquisition of Douglas DC-3 airliners. During 1957 LAV took over Transportes Aereos Centro-Americanos (TACA) de Venezuela.

Today the airline operates a large domestic network of scheduled passenger services. This government-controlled airline took delivery of its first Douglas DC-9, a Series -14 on 23 October 1968, this being YV-C-AAA c/n 47309 f/n 393, and it now operates an all McDonnell Douglas twin-jet airliner fleet comprising one DC-9-15, two DC-9-32, one DC-9-34CF, seven DC-9-51s and six MD-83s, the first of the latter acquired in 1986.

The different size models of the popular Long Beach-built airliner provide seating capacities ranging from eighty-five in the DC-9-15 to 163 passengers in the larger MD-83.

Today the airline's routes serve the regional points of Curacao, Aruba, Barbados, Georgetown, Granada, Havana, Ponte-a-Pitre, San Juan, Santa Domingo, Port of Spain, as well as Orlando, Florida and Atlanta, Georgia in the United States. Domestic routes extend from its base at Caracas to Barcelona, Barinas, Maturin, Porlamar, Puerto Ordaz, Barquisimeto, Acarigua, Maracaibo and many others.

A new style livery was introduced to the LAV fleet during the early 1990s. The upper surface is white, with a dark-blue cheatline on the windowline this having a white pinstripe below. The lower part of the fuselage appears grey. The tail unit is dark blue with an outlined bird motif between two thin bars. The top of the fuselage, well forward, has 'VENEZUELA' small in dark-blue, the national flag, 'AEROPOSTAL' in dark-blue and the bird motif logo. The aircraft registration is on the top of the fuselage near the tail, and the engine nacelles are white with 'DC-9-31' and 'McDonnell Douglas' inscribed.

Seen during 1991 is DC-9-31 YV-24C c/n 47727 f/n 848 delivered to LAV on 17 December 1976. It is named *El Falconiano* and serves the airline today along with six other DC-9-51s. *(MAP)*

MARTINAIR HOLLAND N.V. (MP/MPH/YMP)

The Netherlands

Martinair Holland was formed in May 1958 as Martin's Air Charter, the present title being adopted in 1974. The airline operates worldwide including regular trans-Atlantic passenger services from its base at Schipol, Amsterdam. These operate to Miami, Tampa, Los Angeles, Detroit and Seattle in the United States, to Toronto in Canada, to Puerto Plata and Santa Domingo in the Dominican Republic, Concum in Mexico, Montego Bay in Jamaica and to Holguin in Cuba. Inclusive-tour charters are operated to destinations on the Mediterranean and also to Bangkok, Phuket and U-Taphao in Thailand. Freight contracts form a most important part of the activities of Martinair. Regular cargo services are operated to the Middle and Far East, Australia, Mexico and the United States.

In addition to normal airline and freight cargo activities Martinair maintains and operates the Fokker F.28 used by members of the Dutch royal family and the Dutch cabinet. Third-party maintenance is carried out on the Cityhopper's Fokker 50s and F.28s belonging to KLM. Shareholders are the Royal Nedlloyd Group with 49.2 per cent, KLM with 29.8 per cent and various financial institutions the remaining twenty-one per cent.

Martinair has been a Douglas DC-9 operator since 1 August 1968, when it introduced the first of three DC-9-33RC — rapid change — aircraft on its European and Mediterranean routes. The fleet was later joined by a single DC-9-32 and three leased MD-82s, the latter appearing in 1981. The company provides DC-9 line maintenance to several airlines at its base at Schipol airport. When the DC-9 was introduced into service a very distinctive livery was chosen, this consisting of a white top, with a blue cheatline on the windowline bordered by a red pinstripe, the nose section being red. The tail unit was striped with an equal number of red and blue lines, all with a white pinstripe border and a white oval in which appeared 'MAC' in dark blue. The title 'MARTINAIR HOLLAND' appeared on the fuselage top with the Martinair proud, whilst the aircraft registration and the Dutch national flag appeared towards the rear of the fuselage. The lower portion of the fuselage and the engine nacelles were natural metal with a chevron design of red and blue and a styled 'DC-9' inscription.

Today Martinair, despite having neither DC-9 or MD-80 on its fleet inventory still operates the Douglas DC-10 and has the new McDonnell Douglas MD-11 on order for delivery in 1995. Seen in flight over the Californian terrain is DC-9-33RC PH-MAN c/n 47291 f/n 343 on a pre-delivery test flight. It was delivered on 21 July 1968, and was named *Karel de Grote/Charlemagne*. On 1 November 1973, it was sold via the Chase Manhattan Bank to Hawaiian Airlines being registered N94454 and delivered from Amsterdam on 6 October 1973. On 21 October 1978 it was leased by Hawaiian to Itavia. Today this airliner is in service with ABX Air Inc., better known as Airborne Express, and registered N933AX. *(MDC)*

MIDWAY AIRLINES (ML/MID)

United States of America

Midway Airlines was formed in 1976 to operate scheduled passenger services from Chicago's Midway Airport, and commenced low-fare single-class services on 1 November 1979. It initially utilised a small fleet of three sixty-three seat twin-jet Douglas DC-9-14s acquired from Trans World Airlines, these being N1055T c/n 45736 f/n 45, N1056T c/n 45737 f/n 49 and N1067T c/n 45781 f/n 101. The initial service was soon upgraded to a business orientated class service called 'Metrolink'. Routes served included Minneapolis/St. Paul, Omaha, Kansas City, St. Louis, Columbus, Washington DC., Philadelphia, New York, Boston, Cleveland, Tampa, Detroit, Topeka, Lincoln and Dallas/Fort Worth. Following the demise of Air Florida, Midway established a new subsidiary in 1984 called Midway Express operating former Air Florida equipment including Douglas DC-9s and routes.

By the end of the first year of operations the number of DC-9s had increased to seven. The commutor carrier Fischer Bros. Aviation was acquired in May 1987, this operating as Midway Commutor. By March 1990 Midway was providing scheduled passenger services to no less than fifty-four destinations from hubs at its home base of Midway, Chicago, and Philadelphia. The latter hub was opened on 15 November 1989, with flights serving Sarasota, Tampa, West Palm Beach, Albany, Buffalo, Boston, Hartford-Springfield.

Soon the Midway network was greatly expanded to serve more than sixty destinations in the United States, Canada, the US Virgin Islands and the Bahamas. Commensurate with this rapid expansion Midway added more Douglas twin-jets to its fleet, all of which were fitted out with eight first class seats. At one period, the airline boasted one of the highest utilisation rates of any Douglas DC-9/MD-80 operator at over eleven hours. The October 1991 aircraft inventory from McDonnell Douglas listed thirty-nine DC-9s on the Midway inventory, these being made up of DC-9-15 and DC-9-30 airliners.

Midway Airlines ceased operations on 14 November 1991, prior to completion of a deal whereby the airline was to be bought by Northwest. This failed, leaving 4,300 employees jobless. Despite becoming the 12th largest airline in the USA., Midway just could not compete with the larger airlines that offered more flights to more destinations. It had grown steadily into a $655 million-a-year operator.

The original livery of Midway was most colourful and included a white fuselage top, with dull metal lower surface. The cheatline extending from nose to tail consisted of orange, red, yellow and blue, the blue broadening out to envelope the tail unit and rear of the upper fuselage. An airline motif in a part orange circle was made up of a arrowhead design and this decorated the tail unit. The title 'Midway' appeared forward on top of the fuselage, and the engine nacelles were dark blue, carrying the aircraft registration in white.

Depicted during a pre-delivery test flight is DC-9-15 N1067T c/n 45781 f/n 101 originally delivered to TWA on 11 April 1967. It was sold to Midway in 1979 and was still in airline service when the company folded suddenly in November 1991. (MDC)

MIDWEST EXPRESS (YX/MEP/XYX)

United States of America

Midwest Express, a US scheduled carrier, is a subsidiary of K-C Aviation, which, in turn, is a subsidiary of Kimberly-Clark Corporation, a major consumer products company, the maker of Kleenex and Huggies, with 45,000 employees worldwide. Commencing in 1948, Kimberly-Clark provided corporate transportation for its executives travelling between headquarters and company mills. The expertise in operating a corporate air service led in 1969 to the formation of K-C Aviation, offering aircraft customising and aviation services to corporate clients. After the US airline deregulation act of 1978, Kimberly-Clark and K-C Aviation decided to capitalise on their decades of aviation expertise through the formation of a commercial air carrier — Midwest Express Airlines. During 1982 the company purchased a single Douglas DC-9-14 twin-jet airliner to operate as a corporate aircraft. The company then purchased a small fleet of DC-9s and commenced flying non-stop services from its hub at the General Mitchell International Airport at Milwaukee, Wisconsin. Today it serves Appleton, Atlanta, Bloomington/Normal, Boston, Chicago, Cleveland, Columbus, Dallas/Fort Worth, Denver, Des Moines, Detroit, Flint, Grand Rapids, Green Bay, Indianapolis, Kalamazoo, Kansas City, La Crosse, Lansing, Los Angeles, Louisville, Madison, Muskegon, New York/La Guardia/Newark, Preoria, Philadelphia, Rochester, Rockford, Saginaw, San Diego, San Francisco, Washington DC. and Wausa/Stevens Point. Tampa and Fort Lauderdale in Florida are also served. Operations commenced on 11 June 1984.

The General Mitchell Airport is also the home of the Midwest Express maintenance facility utilising a 60,000 sq ft state-of-the-art hangar built in 1988. At Milwaukee the airline employs 850 of its 1,000 airline personnel and has earned its reputation as "The care in the air" by offering its passengers luxury service at coach fares or less. Catering for the business traveller the airline operates eight DC-9-14/15 aircraft in a two-by-two luxury configuration seating sixty in extra wide leather-covered seats. Three of the four larger DC-9-32s are fitted out to accommodate eighty-four passengers. Shuttle flights as required are operated for the parent company, and more recently two MDC MD-88s were put into service.

The airline is unique in that it has in its fleet DC-9-14 N700ME c/n 45696 f/n 2 which it purchased on 25 September 1986. Previous owners included Skybus, Southern, Spantax, Best and Delta, the latter accepting delivery from Douglas on 17 July 1966, after its participation in an extensive flight test programme with the maker. When Midwest purchased the veteran DC-9 it had accumulated 53,088 hours and accomplished 56,742 landings. During a refurbishment programme that required nearly twenty weeks and 30,681 labour hours, the airliner was stripped of all systems and components, including its interior, cabin and cargo flooring insulation, all removable structures, flight controls and avionics, plus engines were replaced. A new paint finish and a new cabin interior completed the programme. Also a veteran in the Midwest fleet is N500ME c/n 45711 f/n 4, a DC-9-14 initially delivered to Air Canada as CF-TLB on 12 April 1986. It was previously registered N85AS.

Depicted at General Mitchell International Airport, Milwaukee, Wisconsin is DC-9-14 N700ME c/n 45696 f/n 2, the veteran of the Midwest Express fleet, waiting to board passengers. The refurbishment programme cost $430,000 in materials alone, and today this aircraft is as operative as the day it was delivered initially from Long Beach on 19 July 1966, to Delta. (Midwest Express)

NORTHWEST (NW/NWA)   United States of America

Northwest Airlines was founded in August 1926 as Northwest Airways and from its base in Minnesota soon penetrated westwards into North Dakota and Montana. During 1934 the title Northwest Orient Airlines was adopted and it operated a route from Chicago to Seattle, introducing Lockheed 14s in September 1937, and Douglas DC-3s in March 1939. In June 1945, after having served the US government and war effort in various northern and the Pacific theatres of operations during World War 2, the Civil Aeronautics Board awarded an extension of the main route from Milwaukee to New York, via Detroit. This made Northwest a fourth trans-continental airline although it did not serve the major Californian market. A second arm to this northern service was added in March 1948 when Washington State was served by way of Detroit, Cleveland and Pittsburgh. The company was reorganised in 1985 to form NWA Inc,. a holding company for Northwest Airlines and several other subsidiaries. The following year, in 1986, the airline merged with Republic Airlines.

Major domestic traffic hubs for Northwest are located at Detroit, Michigan; Minneapolis/St.Paul, Minnesota, and Memphis, Tennessee. The airline operates an extensive network of scheduled passenger and cargo services within the United States and Canada, whilst many trans-Atlantic and trans-Pacific destinations are served including many in Europe. With 40,000 employees Northwest operates a diverse fleet of modern airliners built by Boeing, Douglas and Airbus Industries. The McDonnell Douglas aircraft inventory for 31 March 1992, indicates that it operates 146 Douglas DC-9s, eight MD-80s, and twenty-eight DC-10s. The DC-9 fleet includes thirty-eight DC-9-10s, seventy-seven DC-9-30s, one DC-9-40 and twenty-eight DC-9-50 twin-jet airliners. The airline inherited a large fleet of DC-9s when it took over Republic Airlines on 12 August 1986.

Currently Northwest operates the Long Beach-built twin-jets in a number of mid-sized markets from its three major domestic hubs in the USA. All models are configured in a two-class layout, with seating ranging from seventy-eight in the smaller DC-9-10 to 143 in the larger and very popular MD-82. Now one of the world's largest airlines, Northwest operates a fleet of 320 aircraft, with a further 180 on order.

Early in 1992 the Northwest livery was changed. A broad battleship grey fuselage band is the main feature of the new livery, this being just above wing level. The top of the fuselage and the tail unit are scarlet. The airline motif is white and appears on the tail unit, this being an 'N' in a circle with a pointer indicating a northwest direction. The title 'NORTHWEST' is in white on the forward fuselage on the grey cheatline. The under surface of the aircraft is white and a small US national flag is painted on the forward fuselage aft of the cockpit. The Northwest fleet number is under the cockpit and appears again at the rear of the fuselage. The aircraft registration is white, forward of the grey engine nacelles on the fuselage.

Depicted is DC-9-32 N3991C c/n 47175 f/n 298 which was initially delivered to Delta as N3334L on 28 April 1968. It was previously with ALM Antillean Airlines as PJ-SNE and today is part of the huge Northwest fleet of Douglas twin-jet airliners and carries the Fleet No.9942. *(MAP)*

NORTH CENTRAL AIRLINES (YNC)

United States of America

North Central Airlines came into being on 16 December 1952, when it was renamed from Wisconsin Central Airlines which was founded on 15 May 1944, initially operating Lockheed Electra airliners, with Douglas DC-3 airliners following during 1951. The airline operated a large network of routes covering Wisconsin state and linking the twin-cities of Minneapolis/St. Paul with Chicago. It soon became listed as a US major regional scheduled carrier.

In the mid 1960s North Central was ready to join the jet age, having three choices: the British BAC-111, the Douglas DC-9 and the Boeing 737. The choice was the DC-9 and in July 1965 the airline took the plunge and ordered five 100-passenger DC-9s which cost $20 million, and took an option on five more. Douglas was to deliver three of the new airliners in 1967, and two more in 1968. In the meantime six more Convair 440s were purchased bringing the Convair fleet up to thirty, and the remaining sixteen DC-3s were utilised as all-cargo aircraft.

The airline took delivery of its first DC-9-31 on 28 July 1967, this being N951N c/n 47067 f/n 143 and two of these Long Beach-built airliners inaugurated jet services to seventeen cities on 8 September 1967. Experiencing rapid growth, due largely to North Central providing an expanding jet service to major markets, the route network soon reached almost one hundred cities in the United States and neighbouring Canada.

Based at Minneapolis/St. Paul, North Central's strength lay in its ability to link medium-sized cities with major metropolitan areas.

The DC-9-31 fleet eventually reached thirty aircraft, joined with effect from 16 April 1976, by twenty-eight of the newer and bigger DC-9-51s. On 1 July 1979, North Central combined with Southern Airways to form Republic Airlines. Ten of the DC-9-51s mentioned were delivered from the Douglas Aircraft Company at Long Beach after the merger.

The livery for the North Central DC-9s was easily identified by the 'Herman' mallard duck logo which was a feature on the tail unit of the entire fleet. It had been in use since 1947. The silhouetted mallard was encircled by a ring which symbolized the sun by day and the moon by night. The upper aircraft surface was white with the title 'NORTH CENTRAL' taking up most of the fuselage top. A light green cheatline covered the windowline, and below it a white and blue thin pinstripe, the latter with a white border and enlarged aft of the cockpit. The aircraft registration appeared in white on the cheatline at the rear of the fuselage. The lower fuselage was light grey, and the engine nacelles natural metal with 'DC-9' and 'McDonnell Douglas' inscribed.

Depicted is DC-9-51 N760NC c/n 47708 f/n 813 delivered to North Central on 6 April 1976. Today it is part of the huge fleet of DC-9s operated by Northwest and by 15 July 1979 it had flown 8,148 hours and accomplished 13,038 landings. No less than twenty-seven ex-North Central DC-9-51s today serve Northwest. The DC-9 is seen on a pre-delivery test flight from the Long Beach factory over the foot-hills of the Sierra Nevada mountains. (MDC)

OZARK AIR LINES   United States of America

Ozark Air Lines was founded on 1 September 1943, and originally operated inter-state services from Springfield, Missouri, acquiring most of the routes awarded to Park Air Transport. It operated Douglas DC-3 airliners and operated its first service on 26 September 1950, on routes radiating from its headquarters in St. Louis, Missouri, to Chicago, Tulsa and Memphis. By the autumn of 1958 it was operating a fleet of veteran DC-3s numbering twenty. The US airline fleet listing for 31 December 1969, lists Ozark as operating four DC-3s, five DC-9-10s, seven DC-9-30s and twenty-one Fairchild-Hiller FH-227 airliners. It was on 21 January 1965 that the airline announced its plan to acquire three Douglas DC-9-15 twin-jet airliners, and in that same year Ozark carried one million passengers for the first time over a wide network that served fifty-eight cities in sixteen states, mostly in the midwest and the District of Columbia. The first Ozark DC-9-15 was N970Z c/n 45772 f/n 30 delivered to St. Louis on 25 May 1966, with service commencing on 8 July. This first order for the Long Beach-built airliners was doubled six months later, and on 25 November 1965, a third order for three more was placed, this time for the stretched DC-9-31, which carried ninety-five dual-class passengers instead of seventy-five as in the previously ordered models. More orders for both new and second-hand airliners followed and eventually the Ozark DC-9 fleet reached a total of fifty, this including thirty-six DC-9-30s, seven DC-9-15s, three

DC-9-41s and four of the new McDonnell Douglas MD-82s. Apart from its own aircraft, Ozark also operated and maintained the Hugh Heffner Playboy Enterprises DC-9-32 N950PB c/n 47394 f/n 458. In November 1976, the airline embarked on a major cabin conversion programme, equipping all of its DC-9-30s with a 'wide-body' look. This included the fitting of enclosed overhead lockers, soft indirect fluorescent lighting, sculptured ceiling panels and re-covered decorative passenger seats. During September 1986 Ozark Air Lines and its large Douglas DC-9 fleet was absorbed by Trans World Airlines (TWA).

A new livery was introduced on the later series of DC-9 airliners operated by Ozark, but retaining the well-known swallow bird symbol first introduced on its DC-3s in the 1950s. Having a mostly white overall finish to the DC-9-30s they had two green cheatlines on the white border low on the fuselage, with the lower portion being light grey. Above the windowline a broad green cheatline with green pinstripe commenced after the airline title on the forward fuselage top. The white tail unit had a green square containing three white swallow symbols of varying sizes with the title 'OZARK' in white. The engine nacelles were natural metal and the aircraft registration appeared in black on a grey background.

Seen on a pre-delivery test flight from Long Beach is Ozark DC-9-34 N928L c/n 48124 f/n 954 delivered on 10 June 1980. Today this airliner is still in service with Trans World Airlines along with others from the Ozark fleet. *(MDC)*

PURDUE AIRLINES   United States of America

Purdue Airlines was formed on 12 May 1942, as Purdue Aeronautics Corporation, an affiliation of Purdue University assisting activities in support of the school of aviation technology. This Lafayette, Indiana-based US airline operated charter services out of Purdue University Airport to points throughout the United States and Canada. During 1949 it had operated a temporary local service to Chicago, this expiring on 30 January 1950 on inauguration of the service by Turner Airlines. The US airline fleet listing for 31 December 1969 reveals that Purdue had on inventory four Douglas DC-3s, three DC-4s and DC-7s and three Douglas DC-9-30 airliners. The airline had acquired a new DC-9-32 N393PA c/n 47392 f/n 447 on 3 February 1969 and quickly built the fleet up to four aircraft, which included the ex-Hugh Heffner Playboy DC-9-32 N950PB c/n 47394 f/n 458.

Continuing financial difficulties forced the airline to suspend its supplement charter activities in May 1971, and the fleet of DC-9 twin-jet airliners were sold, with the last joining the Ozark Airlines fleet at St. Louis, Missouri, on 11 October 1972.

Purdue Airlines adopted an attractive airline livery utilising a white top to the DC-9, with a pale blue broad cheatline at windowline level. The lower fuselage had a pale grey metal finish. The pale blue tail unit carried a styled 'P' in a white circle and outline. Lower on the tail appeared 'DC-9' and 'McDonnell Douglas' whilst the title 'PURDUE AIRLINES' appeared on the forward fuselage top. The engine nacelles were light blue carrying the aircraft registration in white.

Depicted is DC-9-32 N393PA c/n 47392 f/n 447 seen on the runway at Purdue University Airport at Lafayette, Indiana, the home base of the airline. This particular DC-9 later went to Jugoslavia and was re-registered YU-AJB. *(MDC)*

REPUBLIC AIRLINES (RC/) United States of America

Republic Airlines was formed on 1 July 1979, through the merger of North Central Airlines, based at Minneapolis/St.Paul in Minnesota, and formed in 1948, and Southern Airways based in Atlanta, Georgia, and founded in 1943. Both were well-established major regional airlines and operations under the new title commenced on 1 July 1979, the day of the merger. The new airline was publicly-owned by 42,000 stockholders.

Soon Republic reached the distinction of becoming the world's eighth largest passenger carrier, with in excess of 1,000 daily departures from over one hundred points across the continental United States and extending into Canada, Mexico and the Grand Cayman islands. What became the largest fleet of Douglas DC-9 twin-jet airliners in the world came from the aircraft inherited from North Central Airlines and Southern Airways, as well as from Hughes Air West, which Republic acquired on 1 October 1986.

As of 30 March 1985, Republic based at Minneapolis/St. Paul in Minnesota, had on inventory a fleet of airliners consisting of fifteen Boeing 727-200s, fifteen Convair Cv.580 turbo-prop airliners, thirty-three Douglas DC-9-10s, sixty DC-9-30s, twenty-eight

DC-9-50s, and eight McDonnell Douglas MD-80s. The latter airliners joined the Republic fleet between August 1981 and August 1983. On 12 August 1986, the huge Republic fleet was transferred to Northwest Airlines following a merger.

The Republic livery on the DC-9 consisted of an overall white aircraft with an attractive sky-blue cheatline running above and below the windowline, the upper one having a dark-blue pinstripe border, the lower border being broader, all extending from nose to tail. The title 'REPUBLIC' is contained in a break in the upper cheatline, aft of the cockpit. The trailing edge of the all white tail unit is light-blue. The airline relic from North Central days, 'Herman' the mallard duck insignia, created in 1947, appeared in light-blue on the tail unit. The engine nacelles were natural metal with a small US national flag imposed. The aircraft registration appeared just forward of the engines on the fuselage on the lower sky blue cheatline and the fleet number appeared on the nose. Depicted is DC-9-51 N779NC c/n 48101 f/n 931 ex-Central Airlines, delivered on 7 December 1979, and seen resplendent in new Republic colours. The fleet number is '870'. *(MDC)*

SAS — SCANDINAVIAN AIRLINES SYSTEM (SK/SAS)

Denmark, Norway, Sweden

SAS is the national flag carrier of Denmark, Norway and Sweden and was formed in 1946. In the first few years after World War 2 when British European Airways was rising to leadership in European regional air transport, with Air France in second place, a third airline came to prominence. Its strength had not been foreseen because it represented a bold experiment in international airline co-operation which was without parallel. This was the consortium of companies representing Denmark, Norway and Sweden, forming the Scandinavian Airlines System (SAS). The owners are Det Danske Luftfartselskoep A/S (Danish Airlines); Det Norske Luftfartselskoep A/S (Norwegian Airlines) and AB Aerotransport (Swedish Airlines). It was only after lengthy negotiations that agreement was finally reached on 31 July 1946 for the formation of SAS, demanding revolutionary concessions by all parties, and there were naturally a number of legal complications.

The history of the airline reveals that it has been a profitable operator of most of the Douglas Commercial types produced over the years. It has also been a prolific operator of the McDonnell Douglas twin-jet airliner since it first introduced into its fleet the DC-9-41 LN-RLK c/n 47116 f/n 308 on 14 May 1968. This airliner, by 22 August 1975, had flown 17,706 hours and accomplished 17,357 landings. The DC-9-41 was built specifically to SAS requirements for an aircraft to service its extensive short-haul network. Between 1968 and 1979 SAS acquired forty-nine DC-9-41 twin-jets. Another Long Beach-built model for SAS was the 'hot and high' DC-9-21 taking delivery of the first — LN-RLL c/n 47301 f/n 382 — on 22 March 1969. The airline bought two DC-9-33F for its cargo services, and later supplemented its fleet with DC-9-32s and DC-9-51s, making SAS unique in that it operated every Douglas DC-9 model with the exception of the smaller DC-9-10.

Today operating Europe's largest fleet of McDonnell Douglas aircraft, SAS had on inventory thirty-four DC-9-41s and nine DC-9-21s, all of the latter unique in having Danish registrations, four being previously registered in Sweden and two in Norway. During 1983 board approval was given for the current colourful SAS livery, in preference to two similar designs submitted. An overall white fuselage has a striking rhombus in the three national colours of the participating nations, Denmark, Norway and Sweden in that sequence. A simple 'SCANDINAVIAN' title is on the fuselage, forward and above the windowline in dark blue and this colour applies to the 'SAS' on the tail unit. The three national flags appear on the engine nacelles, and the aircraft registration is applied on the fuselage below the windowline forward of the engines. The three national flags appear on the white engine nacelles.

Depicted is DC-9-21 SE-DBO c/n 47361 f/n 488 delivered to SAS on 1 May 1969, and named *Siger Viking*. It has been registered OY-KIC and also leased to Nordic East. *(MAP)*

SAUDI ARABIAN AIRLINES (SV/SVA)

Saudi Arabia

Saudi Arabian Airlines is the national airline of the Kingdom and currently the largest carrier in the Middle East. The airline was formed at the end of 1946 and commenced its first service on 14 March 1947. It is owned by the Saudi Arabian government and initially received technical aid from the US Air Force and from Trans World Airlines (TWA) with whom it had a contract. The airline operates scheduled passenger and cargo services to twenty-four domestic and fifty-one international destinations.

Today the fleet is large and varied including in its inventory the Airbus A300, Boeing 747, Lockheed L.1011, McDonnell Douglas DC-8, Grumman Gulfstream, Dassault Falcon, Cessna Citation and Beech King Air. The head office is located at Jeddah and airline employees number just over 24,000.

During 1967, Saudi Arabian Airlines purchased three new Douglas DC-9-15 twin-jet airliners from Long Beach, these being HZ-AEA c/n 47000 f/n 83 delivered on 8 February 1967; HZ-AEB c/n 47001 f/n 94 delivered on 30 March 1967, and HZ-ZEC c/n 47002 f/n 105 delivered on 29 April 1967. These were employed on the airline's routes from Jeddah, Dhahran and Riyadh to destinations which included Bombay, Karachi, Khartoum, Amman, Baghdad, Bahrain, Beirut, Cairo, Damascus, Doha, Dubai, Kuwait, Muscat, Sana'a, Tripoli and Tunis.

All three DC-9-15s were replaced by Boeing 737 airliners in 1972 and HZ-AEA was sold to Aeropostal in Venezuela and delivered on 16 June 1972, registered YV-03C with 11,761 hours and 13,765 landings on the airframe. This DC-9 is still in service with Aeropostal today. HZ-AEB was sold to the USA as N969Z and was delivered on 3 July 1972, having accumulated 11,814 hours and 14,285 landings. On 8 August 1975 it was delivered to LAV and registered YV-18C, having by this time flown 18,213 hours and accumulated 24,040 landings.

The Saudi Arabian livery involved a mainly all-white airliner, the lower portion being natural metal, and featuring a double sub-divided cheatline arrangement in a shade of green and blue. These were seperated by a narrow gold stripe running through the windowline with each window outlined in gold. The cheatline extended from the nose along the fuselage finally sweeping up to the top of the tail unit. The traditional Saudi logo, basically consisting of two crossed swords in front of a palm tree, appeared in a gold circle on the fin of the DC-9s. On the fuselage the Saudia Arabian national flag preceded the airline title 'SAUDI ARABIAN AIRLINES' in English on the port side, appearing in Arabic on the starboard side. The engine nacelles were decorated with the fuselage colours, and the aircraft registration was carried in black at the rear of the fuselage.

Depicted in flight is DC-9-15 HZ-AEA c/n 47000 f/n 83, this aircraft being still in service today with LAV in Venezuela. When it changed registration to YV-C-ANP on 1 December 1980, it had accumulated 23,732 hours and accomplished no less than 32,832 landings. (MDC)

SERVIVENSA (VC/VE/SVE)   Venezuela

Servivensa is a subsidiary of Avensa (Aerovias Venezolonas SA) and is based in Caracas, Venezuela. The parent company operates domestic scheduled passenger services to numerous destinations in the country, whilst international services are operated to Mexico City and Panama City.

The large internal network covered by Servivensa includes schedules serving Caracas, Maracaibo, Barcelona, Maturin, Ciudad Bolivar, Parlamor, Puerto Ordaz, Barquisimeto, San Antonio and many others. Airliners used are Douglas DC-9 twinjets which were introduced into service early in 1967 when it acquired two new DC-9-14s. Initially the DC-9-32s it later acquired were leased to Midway Airlines.

The McDonnell Douglas aircraft inventory dated 31 March 1992, lists Servivensa as operating five DC-9 airliners under the Avensa title, but there are actually only three used by the subsidiary.

Avensa operates nine Boeing 727-200s, eight 727-100s and two Convair Cv.580 prop-jet airliners. The three DC-9-32s currently on the Servivensa inventory are supplemented by four Douglas DC-3s and three Boeing 727 airliners. The three DC-9-32s are all ex-Delta Air Lines, being registered YV-612C c/n 45710 f/n 100 ex YV-66C, N939ML and N3315L: YV-613C c/n 47104 f/n 220 ex-N910ML and N3325L: and YV-614C c/n 47105 f/n 221 ex-N902ML and N3326L, all initially delivered to Delta during 1967.

Livery for Servivensa is attractive with an all-white aircraft the title 'SERVIVENSA' in black on the forward fueslage top. A black cheatline envelops the windowline, whilst four black stripes cover the nose section. A half-wing airline emblem adorns the tail unit, and a small national Venezuelan flag and the aircraft registration is on top of the rear fuselage by the engines. Depicted is DC-9-32 YV-613C photographed during 1991. *(MAP)*

SOUTHERN AIRWAYS (SO/XSO)

United States of America

Southern Airways of Atlanta, Georgia, was founded during July 1943 but was not certificated until April 1947, this certificate being re-issued on 8 February 1949. It began scheduled services on 10 June 1949, operating a fleet of ubiquitous Douglas DC-3 airliners on the route from Memphis to Atlanta, Charlotte, Charleston in South Carolina, and Jacksonville, Florida. The US airline fleet listing for the autumn of 1958 showed thirteen DC-3s on the Southern Airways inventory. A similar fleet listing for 31 December 1969 showed Southern as operating seven Douglas DC-9-10s and three DC-9-30 twin-jet airliners plus twenty-four other aircraft types which included the Martin 4-0-4 airliner. During the mid-1960s, when most of the local service airliners were re-equipping with propeller-turbine airliners, Southern decided not to operate the type; a distinction which it was probably proud to share with both Pan American and TWA. Also at this time the Civil Aeronautics Board (CAB) proceeded to issue new routes to the smaller airlines including Southern, who obtained several nonstop routes out of the rapidly-growing industrious Huntsville, Alabama.

The airline was unique in that it made a massive leap by re-equipping straight from the Martin 4-0-4 piston-engined airliner to jet aircraft. On 11 May 1967, Southern took delivery of the first of six Douglas DC-9-15 aircraft, this being N91S c/n 47063 f/n 111, the type entering service on 15 June. Twenty more of the early Series 10, including DC-9-14s and DC-9-15RC models, were obtained from the second-hand market over the following years. On 29 April 1969, the first DC-9-31 N89S c/n 47042 f/n 486 joined the fleet.

By the end of 1976 the airline route network had grown so much that Southern was serving no less than fourteen states, the District of Columbia and the US Cayman Islands in the West Indies. It transpired that more that ninety-five per cent of Southern Airways revenue passenger miles were generated aboard its Douglas DC-9 fleet, the type serving fifty-six out of the sixty-three cities on its network. On 1 July 1979, Southern Airways merged with North Central Airlines to form Republic Airlines, and at the time of the merger the Southern fleet consisted of four ninety-six-seat DC-9-31s and twenty seventy-five-seat DC-9-14/15 airliners.

Southern Airways employed a very smart and striking livery for its DC-9 fleet, comprising an all-white finish to the fuselage top and tail unit. The lower part of the airliner was natural metal. A dark navy-blue cheatline enveloped the windowline extending neatly from nose to tail with the aircraft registration in white at the rear with 'DC-9' in white painted just aft of the cabin. The tail unit had two styled symbols, one in dark-blue and yellow, this yellow also fringing the fuselage cheatline. The airline title 'SOUTHERN' in dark-blue was on the forward fuselage top, with the engine nacelles in half blue with yellow pinstripes and half natural metal.

Seen in flight over the beauty of the Californian coastline near the factory at Long Beach is DC-9-31 N89S c/n 47042 f/n 486, the first DC-9 for Southern which carried the Fleet No.930 on the fin. When sold to Republic on 15 July, this airliner had flown 26,654 hours and accomplished 41,396 landings. Today this DC-9 is still in service with Northwest and carries the Fleet No.9930. *(MDC)*

STANDARD AIRWAYS   United States of America

Standard Airways was founded during 1946 as Standard Air Cargo with headquarters in Seattle, Washington state, and was a US supplemental airline with an area of charter operations encompassing the continental United States, Canada, Mexico and the Caribbean. Operations were suspended on 31 January 1964, but resumed again under the direction of Frank B. Lynott on 17 July 1966, utilising an ex-QANTAS Boeing 707-138 aircraft. It received overseas operating authority for Canada and Mexico on 15 December 1966.

In November 1966 it added to its fleet of Boeing 707s, two Douglas DC-9-15 twin-jet airliners, acquired new from the manufacturer at Long Beach. These included N490SA c/n 45798 f/n 59 delivered on 3 November 1966, and N491SA c/n 45799 f/n 69 delivered on 30 November 1966. The DC-9s were operated for

two years before being sold to Ozark Air Lines of St. Louis, Missouri, on 1 October 1968. On 24 September 1969 Standard Airways ceased operations.

The livery for the Standard Airways DC-9s consisted of a white fuselage top and sides with a natural metal undersurface. A gold-coloured cheatline extended on the windowline from nose to tail, with the aircraft registration in black near the tail. The all-white tail unit carried a large 'S' in gold, and the airline title 'STANDARD' was in red on the forward fuselage top. The engine nacelles were half gold, half white.

Depicted on a pre-delivery test flight is the first DC-9 for Standard, a DC-9-15 N490SA c/n 45798 f/n 59, seen in the vicinity of the Douglas Aircraft Company factory, located at Long Beach in southern California. (MDC)

SUDFLUG (ZSF/)

Germany

Suddeutsche Fluggesellschaft (Sudflug) was founded during 1962, and operated charter services in the mid 1960s untilising Douglas DC-8 and DC-9 aircraft. Two new Douglas DC-9-32 twin-jet airliners were delivered new from the Douglas factory at Long Beach. These were D-ACEB c/n 47218 f/n 312 delivered on 21 May 1968, and D-ACEC c/n 47219 f/n 325 delivered on 13 June 1968. Unfortunately the two DC-9s remained in Sudflug service for only five months, as the airliner succumbed to financial pressures and was merged into Condor, another German operator, on 1 January 1969. Both Douglas DC-9-32s went to Swissair during October 1968, with D-ACEB becoming HB-IFX on 20 October with 1,300 flying hours and having accumulated 1,733 landings. The Douglas archives reveal that this DC-9 was sold by Swissair to Texas International in the United States, being delivered as N538TX on 15 February 1982, by which time it had flown 31,816 hours and accomplished 35,751 landings. Continental Airlines took over Texas International, so on 31 October 1982 N538TX went to Continental

with a total of 33,611 hours flown and 37,315 landings. Today this DC-9 is still in service with Continental Airlines and carrying the fleet No.538.

Sudflug adopted a white top for its DC-9s with a dark-blue cheatline enveloping the windowline and extending from nose to tail. A thin pinstripe ran below the cheatline. The tail unit was dark-blue overall decorated with a circle of ten stars in which was a styled eagle-type logo. Below this was a horizontal double pinstripe in white. The fuselage top had the airline title 'SUDFLUG' in dark-blue well forward, whilst the aircraft registration and German national flag were well aft. The engine nacelles were half dark-blue with pinstripe and half natural metal.

Depicted in flight over the lower Sierra Nevada mountain slopes on a pre-delivery test flight from Long Beach is DC-9-32 D-ACEB c/n 47218 f/n 312. The archives reveal that this airliner is today in service with the large fleet operated by Continental with whom it is registered N538TX, and it is operated on a lease from the Aviation Sales Company. *(MDC)*

SWISSAIR (SR/SWR)   Switzerland

Swissair was formed on 26 March 1931 by the amalgamation of Ad Astra Aero and Basle Air Transport (Balair), becoming Swiss Air Transport Company — Swissair. Ad Astra was formed as early as 1919, commencing flying-boat operations in Switzerland prior to pioneering international routes. Today the airline operates an extensive network of scheduled passenger and cargo services, linking no less that 109 cities in 64 countries in Europe, North and South America, Africa and the Middle East. The fleet as of March 1992 consisted of the Airbus A310-221, A310-322, Boeing 747-357, 747-357 Combi, Fokker 100, Douglas DC-10-30, DC-10-30ER, McDonnell Douglas MD-81 and the new MD-11.

One of the first airlines to operate the Douglas DC-9-10 twin-jet airliner, Swissair took delivery of five DC-9-15 between 20 July 1966, and 26 June 1967. The first was HB-IFA c/n 45731 f/n 34 named *Graubunden* and delivered on 20 July 1966. These were soon supplemented and later replaced by the larger and more popular DC-9-30, with Swissair eventually operating twenty-nine different aircraft including one DC-9-33F all-cargo version HB-IFU c/n 47384 f/n 543 *Payerne* delivered on 22 October 1969 and placed in service on 1 November. During 1974-75, two DC-9-41s were leased from SAS before Swissair expanded its Douglas twin-

jet fleet further with the DC-9-51. The airline took delivery of the first DC-9-50 Series aircraft c/n 47654 f/n 757 first flown at Long Beach on 17 December 1974, as N54641. It was delivered to Swissair as HB-ISK *Hori* and it was the Swiss national carrier who originated the airline requirement for this higher-capacity airliner with an order for twelve aircraft.

The livery adopted by Swissair was distinctive on the DC-9 fleet with the Swiss national flag occupying the complete tail unit. This was complemented by red 'SWISSAIR' titles on a white fuselage top. A red cheatline covered the windowline this having a white pinstripe below. The lower fuselage and engine nacelles were natural metal and the aircraft registration was in white on the red cheatline at the rear of the fuselage.

Depicted is DC-9-32 HB-IFZ *Dubendorf* c/n 47479 f/n 605 seen on a pre-delivery test flight from Long Beach. It was delivered on 18 September 1970, and placed in service on 26 September. Its last service with the airline was on 11 May 1979, and it was then sold to Balair on 18 May. Today this DC-9-32 is in service in the United States with Northwest Airlines, registered N985US Fleet No.9985 and leased from Intercredit. *(MDC)*

TEXAS INTERNATIONAL AIRLINES (TI/XTI)

United States of America

Texas International was known until 1968 as Trans-Texas Airways, formed originally as Aviation Enterprises and commencing scheduled services on 11 October 1947. By August 1958 Trans-Texas was operating a fleet of twenty veteran Douglas DC-3 airliners. The airline based at Houston, Texas, founded on 14 November 1944 as Trans-Texas Airways, was certificated on 12 May 1947, with the original route being operated from Houston to San Antonio and Dallas with extensions mainly in the south Texas area. Initially the airline served eight cities in Texas with its fleet of DC-3s, the first two of which were acquired from American Airlines.

During the early 1960s, like many of the local service carriers, Trans-Texas operated the popular Convair Cv.340. Later with the introduction of the propeller turbine engine many of these were given a new lease of life. Both Allison in the USA and Rolls-Royce in the United Kingdon were producing the new engines. Trans-Texas elected to do its own conversion of its Convair Cv.340s fitting Rolls-Royce Dart turbo-props, the airliners being re-designated Convair Cv.660s. The first was put into service by Trans-Texas on 1 March 1966.

On 30 October 1966 Trans-Texas introduced the eighty-seat Douglas DC-9-14 twin-jet airliner onto its routes from Dallas and Houston to Harlingen, McAllen, Monterey, Tampico and Veracruz. This airliner, N1301T c/n 45696 f/n 2, was delivered to the airline on 30 September 1966. Trans-Texas became the only airline to purchase the DC-9-15MC convertible model, taking delivery of five of the series between September 1967 and January 1968. The first one was N1303T c/n 47044 f/n 165, delivered on 28 September 1967, and the fifth was N1307T c/n 47062 f/n 223, delivered on 26 January 1968.

In 1968 Trans-Texas Airways was renamed Texas International Airlines and by February 1969 had taken delivery of two DC-9-31s, forerunners of a total fleet of twenty-one aircraft, of which thirteen were purchased new from Douglas at Long Beach. This ninety-nine-passenger version proved a great success on the airline's high density routes. Other second-hand purchases included seven DC-9-14/15s. The complete DC-9 fleet of Texas International offered ninety-five per cent of total seat capacity on its routes in the states of Arkansa, California, Colorado, Louisiana, Mexico, Mississippi, New Mexico, Tennessee and Texas. On 31 October 1982 the Texas Air Corporation, the parent company, merged Texas International Airlines into Continental Airlines.

Texas International adopted a bright and colourful livery for its DC-9 fleet. The fuselage had a white top and light grey lower surface, with the windowline covered by a bright red cheatline extending from nose to tail. Above this was a bright blue cheatline broken by the airline title 'Texas International' followed by the US national flag. This blue extended to the tail unit covering all but the leading edge which was white. A large exploded star in white adorned the tail, whilst the engine nacelles were grey with the aircraft registration in black.

Seen on pre-delivery test flight from Long Beach is DC-9-32 N3509T c/n 47798 f/n 914 delivered to Trans-Texas on 12 July 1979. (MDC)

TRANS-AUSTRALIA AIRLINES (TN/)   Australia

Trans-Australia Airlines (TAA) was formed during August 1945. On 12 February 1946 the Australian National Airlines Commission was appointed, charged with the responsibility of establishing interstate and territorial airline services — a sequel to the passing of the Austrialian National Airline Act on 16 August 1945. On 3 June 1946, Lester Brain was made General Manager of TAA and during the next month a National Airlines School was established near Melbourne. To avoid confusion with the title of Australian National Airways (ANA), the name Trans-Australian Airlines was adopted as the operating title of the new airline.

The initial TAA fleet consisted of eleven converted war-surplus Douglas C-47s, or DC-3s, previously leased from ANA, Qantas, Guinea Airways and MacRobertson Miller Aviation (MMA). A trial service was opened between Melbourne and Sydney on 9 September 1946, and the first public scheduled flights on this route commenced on 7 October four times daily, calling at Canberra. On 4 November the Melbourne to Hobart and Sydney to Brisbane routes were added. Four-engined Douglas DC-4 Skymasters entered TAA service and were used to initiate a night service between Melbourne and Perth, via Adelaide, on 2 December. The airline had wasted very little time, and within three months of the first public flight, all the state capitals were being served.

In 1947 there was further expansion, followed by considerable inroads into the Queensland-route traffic during 1948. On 2 April 1949, TAA took over all the Qantas domestic services including some Flying Doctor operations. With effect from 18 October 1948, the Convair Cv.240 was introduced into service, and the airline became one of the earlier puchasers of the Vickers Viscount airliner and the first turbo-prop service was opened on the Melbourne — Sydney — Brisbane route on 18 December 1954. Being extremely sensitive to equipment quality, TAA was anxious to obtain pure jet airliners as soon as possible.

The first Douglas DC-9-31 service flew its first commercial flight with TAA on 17 April 1967, over the Melbourne — Sydney — Brisbane route. The first aircraft was VH-TJJ c/n 47007 f/n 87 delivered on 18 March 1967. Commencing in November 1981 the airline undertook a major refurbishing programme, upgrading eight of its twelve DC-9-31s with a new 'wide-body' look, new seats, decor and enclosed overhead lockers, as well as improved dual automatic pressurisation system. Disposal of the DC-9 fleet began in 1982, but was slow, its last remaining five aircraft being sold to Australian Aircraft Sales in the autumn of 1989. By this time, with effect from 1986, the airline had become re-titled Australian Airlines.

TAA had intended to use the five DC-9s to form the nucleus of a potential low-fare tourist fleet, but as a result of public reaction to ageing jet aircraft, the airline decided to withdraw the aircraft from its service to Queensland. Short-haul routes were served and included direct flights from Melbourne to Sydney, Launceston, Hobart, Canberra; Sydney to Canberra and Brisbane; Brisbane to Rockhampton and Townsville; Rockhampton to Mackay and Townsville to Cairns.

The TAA DC-9s had a white top to the fuselage, a black cheatline extending the length of the fuselage on the windowline, the rest of the body being natural metal finish. The tail unit was also natural metal and decorated with a large black 'T' and the title 'TAA' in red, 'T-JET' in black, and a red kangaroo were placed forward on the fuselage top. Just forward of the engine nacelles and on the fuselage was the inscription 'DC-9 T-JET' in black. A Royal Mail and the Douglas company logo also appeared on the lower fuselage, well forward. The engine nacelles were natural metal and carried the aircraft registration.

Depicted is DC-9-31 VH-TJJ *Edmund Kennedy* c/n 47007 f/n 87 delivered on 18 March 1967. It was involved in a hi-jack attempt on 8 June 1979, whilst flying between Coolongatta and Brisbane. It is depicted on a pre-delivery test flight off the Californian coastline near the Douglas factory at Long Beach. This airliner was sold in the USA, going to Midway and registered N938ML. *(MDC)*

TRANS WORLD AIRLINES   United States of America
(TW/TWA)

TWA initially known as Transcontinental and Western Air was founded on 16 July 1930, by a merger by Western Air Express and Transcontinental Air Transport. A mail contract was awarded on 25 August 1930, and the first all-air service from New York to Los Angeles under the name of TWA was flown by a Ford Tri-Motor on 25 October 1930, taking thirty-six hours, with an overnight stop at Kansas City. In a famous letter dated 2 August 1932, TWA set out the airline's requirement for an all-metal, three-engined airliner, able to carry twelve passengers in hitherto unmatched comfort, at a cruising speed of 146 mph. The letter was circulated to the US leading aircraft manufacturers including Curtiss-Wright, Ford, Martin, Consolidated and Douglas. What followed is aviation history, and resulted in the first of the Douglas Commercial airliner series, the Douglas DC-1. TWA bought the DC-1 and ordered twenty-five of the production model this becoming the DC-2, enabling the airline to retire its remaining Ford Tri-Motors.

Today TWA, which changed its title to Trans World Airlines on 17 May 1950, is recognised as one of the world's largest airlines, despite its future being in jeopardy due to the world recession in the 1990s. Late in January 1992 it was announced that the corporate raider-turned airline chief, Icahn, was negotiating a reorganisation plan before seeking protection under Chapter 11 of the US Federal Bankruptcy code.

The airline operates an extensive network of scheduled passenger services over trunk routes in the USA and to Europe and the Middle East. In September 1986 TWA absorbed Ozark

Air Lines of St. Louis, and made this Missouri base one of its main operating hubs along with JFK airport at New York. The huge airline fleet consists of the Boeing 727, 747, 767, Lockheed L-1011 Tristar, Douglas DC-9 and McDonnell Douglas MD-80 aircraft. The MDC aircraft inventory for 31 March 1992, includes forty-six DC-9s and twenty-nine MD-80 twin-jet airliners. An order for twenty DC-9-15s was placed with Long Beach in July 1964, these to meet demand on its short to medium length routes, with TWA taking delivery of its first aircraft N1051T c/n 45714 f/n 7 on 25 March 1966. The type proved extremely popular, yet unlike many other major US and foreign carriers, the airline never reordered the later versions of the successful DC-9, but did acquire a large fleet of mixed varients when it absorbed Ozark. Currently on the TWA inventory are seven DC-9-15s, fourteen DC-9-32s, one DC-9-33CF, eighteen DC-9-31s, and two DC-9-34 airliners.

A new colour scheme for TWA was unveiled on 30 November 1974, which replaced the traditional 'twin-globe' scheme. Two red cheatlines commence at the nose of the DC-9 proceeding along the all-white fuselage below the windows. The tail unit displays the TWA logo in white on a red centre section panel. A 'TRANS WORLD' title in red appears on the forward fuselage top, and the aircraft registration is in red at the rear of the fuselage. The engine nacelles are natural metal.

Depicted is DC-9-31 N988Z c/n 47134 f/n 215 leased from Polaris which is active in the current TWA fleet. It is ex-Northeast to whom it was delivered as N980NE on 15 December 1967. *(MAP)*

TRINIDAD AND TOBAGO (BWIA INTERNATIONAL) AIRWAYS (BW/BWA)

Trinidad & Tobago

British West Indian Airways International, the national carrier of the Caribbean islands of Trinidad and Tobago was formed on 1 January 1980, through the merger of BWIA International and Trinidad and Tobago Air Service (TTAS). However, British West Indian Airways (BWIA) was originally formed on 27 November 1939, by a New Zealander, Lovell Yerex. The first operations were with a Lockheed Lodestar, flying between Port of Spain, Trinidad, and Barbados, via Tobago, commencing on 26 November 1940. Control of the airline passed to British South American Airways (BSAA), later BOAC, during 1947. In November 1961, the Trinidad government acquired a ninety per cent holding, followed by the remainder in 1967. BWIA operated international services to North and South America and Europe. TTAS, formed in June 1974 by the government, operated high-frequency shuttle flights linking the two islands of Trinidad and Tobago. The government merged the two carriers to improve efficiency.

Today the airline fleet consists of four Lockheed L-1011 Tri-Star 500s, nine McDonnell Douglas MD-83 twin-jet airliners, and a single Douglas DC-9-51. The airline first became a DC-9 operator during the summer of 1976 when it took delivery of a leased DC-9-51, prior to acquiring four of its own DC-9-51s, together with a DC-9-34CF. The single DC-9-51 in service today is 9Y-TFH c/n 47743 f/n 859 named "Janelle Penny Commission".

Cargo and passenger services are operated from its headquarters located at Piarco Airport, Port of Spain, Trinidad, to Tobago, Georgetown, Aruba, Caracas, Barbados, St. Lucia, Granada, St. Kitts, Antigua, San Juan in Puerto Rico, Kingston, St. Croix, St. Maarten, Curacao, Miami, Toronto, Frankfurt, Zürich, Cologne and London (Heathrow).

The livery of the BWIA fleet includes a distinctive gold cheatline covering the windowline and broadening as it reaches the rear fuselage and covers also the rear part of the tail unit. Underneath this a thin blue line broadens as it reaches the rear of the aircraft, and slopes with white in between. The top of the fuselage is white, the lower surface being polished metal. The BWIA emblem — the steelband motif — is carried on the fin with 'BWIA' in red inscribed. This is repeated on top of the fuselage along with the national flag of Trinidad. The title 'Trindad and Tobago Airways International' is also carried in black on top of the fuselage. The aircraft registration is carried on the white engine nacelles. Depicted is DC-9-51 9Y-TFF c/n 47737 f/n 829 obtained by BWIA from Finnair with whom it was registered OH-LYS and had completed 1,591 flying hours and 2,797 landings. It is depicted on a pre-delivery test flight from Long Beach. (MDC)

TURK HAVA YOLLARI — THY (TK/THY)

Turkey

THY — Turk Hava Yollari — was formed in May 1933, by the Turkish Government as Devlet Hava Yollari. The first service was operated by de Havilland Dragon Rapides flying between Ankara and Istanbul, followed by other domestic routes. The Turkish Ministry of Transportation assumed control of the airline in 1938 and the first international route was opened in 1947 using Douglas DC-3 airliners operating as far as Athens, Greece. During 1955 the first of a fleet of seven de Havilland Herons were delivered for use on domestic routes. The present title was adopted in 1956, when the airline became a corporation.

A major modernisation programme was introduced during 1958 with the acquisition of Vickers Viscounts, these being followed by Fokker F.27 Friendships. Douglas twin-jet services commenced on European routes on 9 July 1968, with the delivery of the first Douglas DC-9-32 — TC-JAB c/n 45774 f/n 336 — one of ten Long Beach-built airliners, of which nine remain in service today. Fitted out for 111 or 115 passengers, the DC-9s are used on busy schedules covering THY's European routes to such destinations as Amman, Athens, Frankfurt, Milan and Munich and on its extensive domestic network taking in Ankara, Antalya, Adana, Diyarbakir, Evsurum, Gaziantep, Istanbul, Izmir, Malatya, Trabzon and Von. The Douglas DC-9s are also frequently leased to Kibris Turk Hava Yollari — Cyprus Turkish Airlines — for its services from Ankara, Antalya, Adana, Izmire and Istanbul to Ercan (Tymbou) airport, east of Nicosia, Cyprus.

During 1991 the airline added Baku, Denizli, Amman, Beirut and Adu Dhabi to its destinations, and added routes to Barcelona, Manchester, Nice and Strasbourg in 1992, all additions to its extensive network of international scheduled services operated to Europe, the Middle East and North Africa with the Douglas DC-9 airliners. The airline also operates charter flights to Germany for Turkish workers, as well as other special charter flights to various cities. In addition to Cyprus Turkish Airlines other subsidiaries include Gunes Express AS, (Sun Express) and Turk Hava Tasimacilgi (Turkish Air Transport).

A new livery was recently introduced which incorporates an all-red tail unit which has a white disc containing the airline's stylised winged bird motif in red. An all-white fuselage has the airline title 'TURKISH AIRLINES' above the forward fuselage windowline in dark blue, preceded by a small Turkish national flag. 'THY' in red is inscribed just forward of the engines above the windowline. The aircraft registration is small on the engine nacelle which is white. Depicted in the new livery is DC-9-32 TJ-JAD c/n 47488 f/n 527 delivered on 27 August 1969, and seen in landing sequence. It is named *Anadolu* . *(Chris Doggett)*

US AIR (US/USA)   United States of America

The name US Air dates from October 1979, but the background of the airline goes back as far as 1938 when it was known as All American Aviation, the original name for Allegheny Airlines. It was founded on 5 March 1937 to pioneer a highly specialised mail service, this incorporating devises for dropping and picking up mail in flight. By this means fifty-eight small communities in Pennsylvania, Delaware, Maryland, West Virginia and Ohio received an air mail service with effect from 13 September 1938. By the time this service ended in June 1949, Allegheny had become a normal certificated local carrier. During 1968 Lake Central Airlines was acquired, and in 1972, Mohawk Airlines, with both Pacific Southern and Piedmont following in 1987. US Air completed the integration of Piedmont Aviation on 5 August 1989, so creating an airline with over 420 jet airliners and more than 48,500 employees.

Today US Air is one of the world's largest airlines, providing scheduled passenger services to 130 destinations located in the USA, Canada, the United Kingdom, Germany, Bermuda and the Bahamas. The parent company of US Air, US Air Group, owns four regional airlines; Henson, Jetstream International, Pennsylvania and Suburban, and has contractual arrangements with eight others, all of which provide US Air Express feeder services. The airline operates from hubs located at Charlotte, Pittsburgh,

Baltimore, Philadephia, Dayton and Syracuse.

Allegheny placed the Douglas DC-9 into service on 1 September 1966, testing the viable market with a single DC-9-14 N6140A c/n 47049 f/n 42 delivered on 29 July. This was supplemented the following year with the first of what is now a fleet of seventy-three Douglas DC-9-31/32s, fitted out for 110 passengers. In June 1974, an order was placed for eight new DC-9-51 twin-jet airliners which entered service between 10 October 1975, and 27 February 1976, the first being N920VJ c/n 47682 f/n 788. The DC-9-30 series are used on the short-to-medium routes of US Air, whilst a fleet of thirty-one MDC MD-80s fly longer semi-transcontinental routes across the USA. Boeing 727s, 737s, 767s, BAe 146s, Fokker 100s and F.28s complete the huge fleet.

The livery of US Air consists of a highly polished natural metal finish, with a crimson fuselage cheatline, below the windowline above the wing level. A black pinstripe acts as a border under the windows. Except for a leading edge strip, the tail unit is blue with three pinstripes and inbetween the lower two is the title 'USAir' in white. On top of the fuselage adjacent the all metal engine nacelles is a US national flag plus the aircraft registration. Depicted is DC-9-31 N997VJ c/n 47336 f/n 500 initially delivered to Allegheny on 27 May 1969. It is still in service with US Air. *(Chris Doggett)*

VIVA AIR (FV/VIV)   Spain

Viva Air (Vuelos Internacionales de Vacaciones) is a joint venture Spanish scheduled and charter carrier formed on 24 February 1988, by Iberia and Lufthansa. The company operates passenger services within Europe and to Africa and the Middle East. Routes include Barcelona, Madrid and Malaga to London (Gatwick); Alicante, Malaga and Palma de Mallorca to London (Heathrow); Malaga to Paris (Orly), Frankfurt and Dublin; Palma de Mallorca to Frankfurt, Manchester and Paris (Orly); and Alicante to Paris (Orly). The company is owned ninety-six per cent by Iberia, INI two per cent and Pautner two per cent. The company is based at Palma de Mallorca, Spain.

The current aircraft fleet as of March 1992, consisted of six Boeing 737-300s, three Douglas DC-9-30s which are leased, whilst four more 737-300s are on order. The airline commenced operating the three Iberia DC-9-32s in January 1990. These are EC-BIL *Ciudad de Zaragoza* c/n 47084 f/n 179 delivered to Iberia on 11 October 1967: EC-BIU *Ciudad de Oviedo* c/n 47314 f/n 279 delivered on 28 March 1968, and EC-BPF *Ciudad de Almeria* c/n 47364 f/n 484 delivered on 17 April 1969.

Livery for the Viva Air DC-9s includes an overall white airliner, the tail unit being decorated with what one can only describe as an abstract design. The multi-colour title 'VIVA air' is positioned on the lower forward fuselage whilst the Spanish national flag and the aircraft registration are positioned forward of the all-white engine nacelles on the lower fuselage. Depicted is DC-9-32 EC-BIL. *(MAP)*